Curious Histories of Nice, France

D0063220

CURIOUS HISTORIES OF NICE, FRANCE

Margo Lestz

Boo-Tickety Publishing
London

Copyright © Margo Lestz 2015. All rights reserved.

The right of Margo Lestz to be identified as the author of this work has been asserted in accordance with Section 77 of the Copyright, Designs and Patents Act 1988.

No part of this publication may be reproduced or transmitted in any form or by any means, electronic or mechanical, including photocopying, recording or any information storage and retrieval system, without prior permission in writing from the author.

This book is part of the Curious Histories series.

ISBN paperback: 978-0-9931371-3-6
ISBN MOBI ebook: 978-0-9931371-4-3

Published by
Boo-Tickety Publishing
London

Contents

Introduction

This book is not a guide to Nice in the traditional sense. I won't be mapping out tour routes or recommending restaurants. Others can do that much better than I can.

What I will be doing is recounting stories about the people and events from Nice's past that have helped to form the city's character. These stories are meant to be entertaining as well as informative and to help you better understand the city that I happily call my adopted home.

The book is divided into four parts: Before France, Trail of Tourism, Disaster and Dastardly Deeds, and Taste of Tradition. In each part, you'll find an overview or comment on the subject, followed by several related short stories. Most stories have "What to See" and "Fun Facts" sections at the end with additional information.

I feel very privileged to live in Nice and to be able to explore its history on a daily basis. I hope this collection of stories will help to make your time in Nice more interesting and memorable.

Now, let's dive right in to the fascinating history of Nice.

PART 1:
BEFORE FRANCE

Prehistory

One of the oldest known prehistoric settlements in the world is located in Nice. It's called Terra Amata which means "beloved land." It seems those first inhabitants of Nice camped by the sea and hunted elephants with tools made from stones picked up on the beach. (If there were as many stones on the beach then as there are now, we can imagine they would have had no shortage of tools.)

Greek Nice and Roman Cimiez

The Greeks founded Nice around the fourth century BC. They called this hilltop fortification Nikaia which in Greek means "victorious one." Around the first century AD, when Nikaia was under attack, the Greeks sent word to Rome for help. The Romans arrived and saved the day, then they decided the area was so beautiful, they wanted a city here too. They settled in the hills behind Nice and called their city Cemenelum. Today the area is known as Cimiez and is part of the city of Nice.

For three or four hundred years, Cemenelum was a bustling city with a population that rose to nearly 20,000. Like all good Roman cities, it had a system of thermal baths, a large arena, and an aqueduct to keep the city in water.

Around the fifth century AD the Roman Empire was on its last leg. Barbarian invasions were coming from all sides, and Cemenelum was eventually deserted. Everyone from the hilltop moved down to the fortified city of Nice which continued to flourish (between invasions from neighbors)

Provence — Savoy — France

From the late twelfth century through the fourteenth century, Nice was part of the County of Provence. When a civil war broke out in Provence, Nice joined itself to the Counts of Savoy.

Nice went back and forth between the House of Savoy and France until 1860 when it was definitively joined to France. But we'll read more about that a little bit later..

What to See

♦ Stone Age Museum, Terra Amata – 25 Boulevard Carnot . The museum sits on an actual archeological site. Learn how people lived in this area 400,000 years ago.

♦ Cimiez ruins, 160 Avenue des Arènes – the park of Cimiez has Roman ruins as well as olive trees, flower gardens, a monastery, and views of the city.

Bay of Angels

⌒⦴⌒

Two Legends and a Fish Story

Before this land was inhabited, there was the sea and the impressive bay known as the *Baie des Anges* or "Bay of Angels." If you're wondering how this bay came by such a charming name, two legends and a fish story might be able to explain it:

Legend No. 1 — Adam and Eve

Although many rich and famous tourists visit Nice every year, according to one legend, the first visitors were actually Adam and Eve – yes, the ones from the Bible.

As the story goes, after they were kicked out of Paradise for being naughty, they were standing outside the locked gates looking at their new hostile surroundings. They had no idea where to go or what to do.

Then they heard the sound of rustling wings overhead and looked up to see a band of angels. The heavenly host swooped down, picked them up, and carried them across the waters to a land fronted by a glorious bay. It was as lush and beautiful as the Eden they could no longer enter.

And where do you think Adam and Eve's new home was? It was Nice, France, of course! According to some, that's how the *Baie des Anges* came by its name.

Menton, a city just down the coast from Nice, also claims this legend, with one addition. They say when Eve left the Garden of Eden she took a lemon with her. She was looking for a place worthy of the lovely fruit and when she saw Menton she planted the lemon there. Menton is known for its lemons and has a wonderful lemon festival every year.

So where did Adam and Eve make their home? Well, we can't be sure if they settled in Menton or in Nice, but this is my theory: First, they visited Menton, thought it was beautiful, and planted the lemon. Then they saw that Nice was even more beautiful and decided to make it their home.

Why do I think this? Well, for one thing, their house is still standing in the Old Town. It has a magnificent carved frieze depicting the first couple sporting their fig leaves. They each have some sort of club and it looks like they might be having a domestic quarrel. It's called *La Maison d'Adam et Eve* or "Adam and Eve's house" and is at No. 8, Rue de la Poissonnerie where the street meets Cours Saleya. This house is dated 1584, so *maybe* the first couple didn't really live there. Some say that this club-toting couple represents the original owners of the house who were known for their arguments. Whatever it's meant to symbolize, it's a lovely bit of decoration and easy to miss if you are not looking for it.

Legend No. 2 — Sainte Réparate

If the first legend seems a little far-fetched, how about this one: It has to do with a fifteen-year-old girl called Réparate. She was a Christian from Caesarea, Israel, and a victim of Roman persecution in the year 250.

The Romans tried to burn poor Réparate at the stake, but it started to rain and the fire went out. Then they forced her to drink boiling tar but it seems she had a "cast-iron stomach" and that didn't do the job either. Finally they cut off her head and put her body in a little boat which they set adrift on the Mediterranean Sea.

Angels surrounded the boat and guided it into the same beautiful bay where Adam and Eve had arrived all those years before. The bones of Réparate (now known as Sainte Réparate) are in the cathedral in the Old Town which bears her name... But hang on a minute – according to the cathedral's history, her bones arrived in 1060. Does that mean the poor girl's body was adrift at sea for 800 years? We really can't be sure, but this is another legend explaining why the bay is called the *Baie des Anges*.

A Fish Story

If the above two legends are a bit hard to swallow, how about a fish story? At one time the bay had many angel sharks in it. Don't worry though, the angel shark is a relatively harmless shark with fins shaped like wings and they're no longer found in the waters around Nice. When the fishermen of old saw these winged sea creatures they must have thought they resembled swimming angels. And there you have it, that's the third possible explanation for the name, *Baie des Anges*.

Whether the name came from the angels that transported Adam and Eve, the ones that guided Réparate's boat, or the underwater ones seen by the fishermen, I'm sure we can all agree that it is still a heavenly place

What to See

♦ **Bay of Angels** – Admire the bay from the Promenade des Anglais or from the top of the *Colline du Château* (Castle Hill) for a panoramic view.

♦ **Adam and Eve House** – In the Old Town, 8 Rue de la Poissonnerie where it intersects with Cours Saleya.

♦ **Cathedral, St. Réparate** – In the Old Town, 3 Place Rossetti. This building was built in the late 1600s to replace an older and smaller church. This baroque style cathedral was granted historic monument status in 1906.

♦ **Place Rossetti** – This is a lively square with lots of restaurants and people-watching opportunities. While here be sure to have an ice cream at Fenocchio's. They're known for their unusual flavors such as cactus, tomato and basil, violet, etc. If it can be used to flavor ice cream, you can probably find it here.

Fun Facts

♦ The first legend comes from a long poem called, "A Last Canto to Milton's Paradise Lost" or *Un dernier chant au paradis perdu de Milton* in French. It was written in 1856 by Alexis de Jussieu, a French naturalist and poet. Below are some excerpts (translated by me).

On a calm shore there appears to be another Eden,
Second cradle of the world, where nature smiles.
...
This is the great sea! Mirror that the sun
Likes to gaze into the moment she awakes,
...

Oh! voyagers of today, if ever your steps
Bring you one day to these beautiful shores,
Stay, stay the night, wait for the moment
When the beach sleeps, when in the sky,
Like a new sun, the suspended moon
Ignites this vast expanse of sea.
Nowhere else does the sky have a brilliance so pure:
With its transparency it keeps its azure.

Catherine
Ségurane

❧

Niçoise Laundress Saves the Day

In 1543, the city of Nice consisted of the hill with a fortress on top and the area now known as the Old Town. The entire city was protected by a tall, thick wall with towers strategically placed along it. Although small by today's standards, it was an important seaport belonging to the House of Savoy and the French and Turkish armies joined forces to try to take the city.

But they hadn't counted on meeting one very brave laundry lady who struck fear into their hearts. Catherine Ségurane was a young woman living in Nice at the time. She wasn't considered beautiful, neither was she very ladylike. We might say she was a bit *rough around the edges.*

Cathy worked as a laundress, and rain or shine, she was up at daybreak carrying heavy baskets of laundry down to the Paillon River that flowed just outside the walls of Old Nice.

She would trudge out onto the rocky river-bank with her piled-high baskets, get down on her knees and scrub the clothes on the rocks.  After the washing and rinsing, she would fold the garments then beat them with a big wooden paddle to get out any remaining water. All of this heavy lifting and laundry beating meant that Cathy built up some pretty impressive muscles which would come in very handy later.

On August 15, 1543, Cathy woke to a terrible situation. There were 150 French and Turkish ships in the bay and they were firing on Nice. Not only this, but there were Turkish troops on the ground, attacking the city walls from the back, near the area where Cathy lived and worked.

That day every citizen of Nice became a soldier and they fought with whatever they had at hand to protect their city. So what did Cathy have? She had her big sturdy laundry paddle and the muscles and courage to use it. The Turks were climbing up the walls and one of them was making his way up the tower to plant the Turkish flag and claim victory.

When Cathy saw that crescent-mooned flag going up over her city, she went wild with rage. She let out a scream that was heard over the cannon fire and she ran straight for that Turk, laundry paddle swinging. She whacked him in the head and grabbed the flag as he went flying off the tower. She broke the flagpole over her knee then ripped the fabric to pieces.

Next she did something that was decidedly unladylike. She turned her back to the soldiers below, bent over, lifted up her skirt and showed them a different moon than the one on their flag. Then she took their ripped-up flag and wiped her bottom with it before flinging it down on them. The Turks were horrified by this crazy woman and her desecration of their flag and they ran. Cathy had saved the day!

Unfortunately, Cathy's show of bravery wasn't enough to keep them away. They came back later and occupied the city for a while until reinforcements from Savoy arrived to drive them out. But Cathy became a heroine and to this day she remains an emblem of the courageous Niçois spirit.

What to See

♦ **Monument to Catherine Ségurane,** Rue Sincaire – This bas-relief monument is on part of the old city wall where the tower once stood (the tower where Cathy performed her heroic deed). It was a five-sided tower and the word Sincaire means "five sides" in the Niçois language.

Catherine Ségurane became the patron saint of Nice and every year there is a special service in the Old Town cathedral followed by a ceremony in front of the monument... but don't worry, there's no "mooning" allowed.

The inscription on the monument is in the Niçois language. The plaque in French is roughly translated as:
This monument is the result of an idea put forth in 1858 by the Niçois historian, Jean-Baptiste Toselli, to pay homage to Catherine Ségurane, mythic heroine of the history of the city. During the siege of 1543 by the Franco-Turkish armies, of the fortress of Nice, the last possession of the Duc of Savoy, Charles III (1504–1553), tradition states that a humble laundress named Catherine Ségurane spurred on the citizens of Nice by seizing the Turkish flag, knocking out the standard-bearer with her laundry paddle, and saving the city from being taken.
The event took place on August 15, 1543, and is commemorated each year. Honored since the 17th century by different monu-

ments, statues, and literary works, Catherine Ségurane incarnates for History the spirit of resistance of the Niçois identity.

Fun Facts

♦**Truth or Fiction?** – Whether Cathy was real or not is debated, with historians being of both opinions. The first written record of the incident is dated 65 years after the great battle but the "exposed bottom episode" wasn't *revealed* until 1901.

♦ **Shroud of Turin** – The famous piece of linen bearing the image of a man, that many believe is the burial cloth of Jesus, is today known as the Shroud of Turin. But in the early 1500s, around the time of this battle, it was the "Shroud of Nice." The holy cloth was owned by the House of Savoy, and Charles III, Duke of Savoy, brought it with him when he installed his family and his court in Nice in 1536. The following year, there was a public exposition and the Holy Shroud was hung out the window of the castle tower for the townspeople to gaze upon. It was also paraded through the town in a religious procession. In 1543, the year of the Franco-Turkish attack, the Duke moved his court from Nice taking the Shroud with him.

♦ **Cannonballs** – In that first battle, the Niçois turned back the invading troops, but they didn't go away. They started installing cannons on the three hills surrounding Nice: 25 on Cimiez, 20 on Mont Gros, and 28 on Mont Boron. These cannons, combined with the ones fired from the ships in the bay, sent about 2,200 cannonballs crashing into the city over a four-day period.

The fortress on the hill held strong, but the lower town (current Old Town) was taken on August 22. The invaders sacked the city and took 5,000 people to be sold as slaves. Finally, help arrived from Savoy and the Franco-Turk forces were defeated and the slaves released.

When the Niçois started doing the cleanup, they found they had an abundance of cannonballs. Someone had the idea that they would make nice wall decorations and there are still a few on display that can be seen today.

Where to see cannonballs:

- Old Town – Corner of Rue Droite and Rue de la Loge. Plaque reads: "Cannonball fired by the Turkish fleet in the 1543 siege of Nice in which Catherine Ségurana distinguished herself."
- Old Town – Corner of Rue de l'Abbaye and Rue Colonna d'Istra.
- Place Garibaldi – On the south side of the square, just behind the statue of Garibaldi, is the chapel of Très-Saint-Sépulcre. In the arches at street level you can see three cannonballs placed at the top of three arches. They were added as decoration when these buildings were built, a few hundred years after the siege.

Paillon River

From Floods to Flowers

In the center of Nice, just off Place Massena, you will find a beautiful park with jets of water shooting toward the sky. It's called the *Promenade du Paillon* because it's built on top of the Paillon River.

Everything in this park is designed to remind us of the river that flows below it. The walkways are covered in aquatic-colored stone, and there are jets of water and sprays of mist everywhere. In the children's section, wooden sea-creatures follow the river toward the sea and provide the children a place to climb, swing, and bounce.

You might wonder why the city would want to cover a picturesque, gently flowing river. But the Paillon is not that kind of waterway. Even though the riverbed is very wide (as wide as the garden), most of the time there are only a few small streams of water running through it.

When nineteenth-century tourists saw it, they weren't very impressed. One of them called it an imaginary river. Another said it was the driest part of Nice. The Paillon is probably best known for the paintings of laundresses washing their laundry in the little streams and then spreading it out to dry on the rocks in the river bed – just like Catherine Ségurane had done hundreds of years before. This led the amused tourists to say that the Paillon was only good for drying clothes.

If, however, there was a lot of rain in the hills behind Nice, that "imaginary river" could, and did, turn violent very quickly because of its steep descent into the city. Even though these deluges were infrequent, the risk was so great that in the 1800s watchmen on horses were strategically placed to keep an eye on it. If there was danger they would gallop along the riverbanks crying, "The Paillon is coming...the Paillon is coming." Why? Because the nearly dry riverbed was often full of people and animals. Mostly it was full of Niçoise ladies doing their laundry.

One day in July 1887 was an especially bad day for three of those laundresses. The skies over Nice were clear and blue and the riverbed was full of women doing their washing as usual. But what they didn't notice was that in the hills behind Nice there was a storm brewing.

Suddenly, a wall of water comes roaring through the riverbed. Most of the laundry ladies scramble to safety just in time to see all of their clothes washed away. But three of them are stranded on a little island of gravel in the middle of the swirling muddy waters. A crowd gathers and watches helplessly.

Five men decide to act. One of them is Monsieur Garaccino, the son of one of the trapped women. The five brave men wade out together supporting one another. Even though the water is now only about waist high, the current is very strong and the river is carrying lots of mud, stones and other debris which could easily knock a person down.

The first woman to be rescued is Monsieur Garaccino's mamma, of course. Can you imagine the trouble he would have been in if he had rescued someone else first? Monsieur Garaccino puts Mamma Garaccino on his shoulders and with the help of the other four men, they struggle back to the bridge where a ladder has been attached. Mamma Garaccino climbs to safety and the men turn back toward the island.

The water is rising fast and the other two women stranded on the little island are up to their ankles now. Well, one of them is. Aima, the older of the two, is almost hysterical. She is down on her knees praying at the top of her voice to all of the saints in heaven to save her. The men arrive and again, it's Monsieur Garaccino who does the heavy lifting. Aima, Laundress No. 2, is placed on his shoulders and the five men start back toward the bridge. But they stumble and the current takes them all down into the swirling, debris-filled water. They manage to get back up, but poor Aima had swallowed so much of the muddy water, that she had to be taken to hospital where she was in very serious condition.

But Laundress No. 3 still needs saving, so the very tired men make their way back a third time to the little island. Someone has managed to lead his mule out onto the island and Laundress No. 3 is perched on him. The bystanders see that the men are exhausted and want to do something to help. So they tie a bucket to the end of a rope and cast it out to them. It contains an "energy drink" – a bottle of cognac! After downing the bottle, the men are reinvigorated enough to save Laundress No. 3 and the mule.

Rescuing laundresses is pretty hard work and perhaps that is why the city decided to cover the river. They started in 1867 and little by little the river was hidden from view (the part that runs through the center of Nice anyway). And today, that wide, troublesome riverbed that once divided the city is concealed by the lovely water-themed park that has become the city's heart.

But should we be worried about those torrents which in times past poured over the riverbanks? Well, there's a system of overflow tunnels underneath to take care of excess water and an electronic monitoring system which constantly assures that all is well. So hopefully, the deepest water you will see in the park is the two centimeters in the bottom of the fountain and no more rescues will be necessary.

What to See

◆ **Promenade du Paillon**, Place Massena – This park contains 128 water jets, which can be coordinated with music for "dancing waters" performances, mist platforms, children's playground, and a plot of carnations (see Fun Facts).

◆ **Lycée Massena** – Toward the east end of the park, looking north, you can see a beautiful building with a clock tower. This is a secondary school, Lycée Massena. The building was built as a monastery in the 1600s, but has been a school since the early 1800s. In the beginning, it was the only school for the entire department. Of course, it has had many renovations and additions over the years, making it into the large complex you see today. If Harry Potter had been French, this could have been Hogwarts!

Fun Facts

◆ **Carnations** – At one time, Nice was the flower capital of the world, with the city producing more flowers than all of Holland. The specialty of the Niçois flower producers was the carnation, or *œillet*. At the end of the Promenade du Paillon on the south side there is a plot containing about 2,000 carnation plants in honor of the part this flower played in Nice's history.

In 1764, Tobias Smollett wrote in one of his letters from Nice, explaining how the carnations were shipped:

"I must tell you that presents of carnations are sent from hence, in the winter, to Turin and Paris; nay, sometimes as far as London, by the post. They are packed up in a wooden box, without any sort of preparation, one pressed upon another: the person who receives them, cuts off a little bit of the stalk, and steeps them for two hours in vinegar and water, when they recover their full bloom and beauty. Then he places them in water-bottles, in an apartment where they are screened from the severities of the weather; and they will continue fresh and unfaded the best part of a month."

"œillet"
carnation

Cool Old Town

Natural Air Conditioning

The French Riviera is said to have 300 days of sunshine per year. In the summer, all that sunshine really heats things up and temperatures can soar. But in Nice, if you want to beat the heat, all you have to do is duck into the narrow, winding streets of the Old Town and the temperature drops drastically.

It's not just by chance that the temperature is lower in these streets. The Old Town was designed to keep its cool under the hot Mediterranean sun. It was laid out hundreds of years ago and those ancient architects had some pretty good ideas for keeping cool.

Cool Streets

Since there were no automobiles when the city was built, the streets were made just wide enough for people – and maybe a horse-drawn cart or two. The tall buildings and narrow streets mean the pavement and the sides of the buildings are protected from the fierce sun and stay at a comfortable temperature.

Types of air vents you might see over doors in the Old Town

Cool Interiors

But it's not only the streets that are protected from the heat – many of the buildings actually have an early form of natural air conditioning. Strolling through the Old Town, you will notice many openings fitted with iron grills just above the doors. These charming architectural details are more than just decoration. They are part of a clever system designed to bring in the fresh, cool air from street level. It enters the foyer and then rises up through a narrow central courtyard which has an opening at the top. This creates a column of refreshing air rising through the center of the building. The apartments have windows that open to this interior courtyard and bring in the cool air. How clever is that?

Cool Shutters

On the exterior of the building, the shutters have a part to play as well. They have a central section that can swing outward and upward to catch a breeze when the rest of the shutter is closed to keep out the sun. Other features that help to regulate the temperature of these old buildings are thick masonry walls and high ceilings.

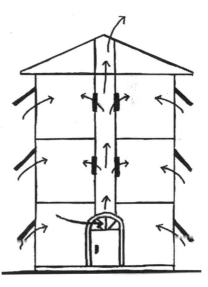

It's pretty impressive that these early architects designed a cooling system that's free, ecological, efficient, and has continued to work for hundreds of years without having to call out the repairman.

What to See

♦ **Air vents** – Stroll through the Old Town and notice the variety of openings over the doorways. Most date from the 1600s to the 1800s.

♦ **Palais Lascaris,** 15 Rue Droite – While wandering around the Old Town looking at cool architecture, you might want to see Palais Lascaris. It was built in the middle of the seventeenth century by the noble Lascaris-Vintimille family. The plain exterior belies the beautiful baroque interior of this stately home that is now a museum with a collection of musical instruments.

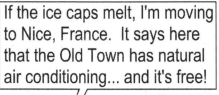

Cours Saleya

Marketing in the Old Town

Cours Saleya is the heart of Old Town Nice where you'll find the lively daily market. Striped awnings cover its center and shelter the products on offer. Crowds of locals and tourists come here to do their shopping or just to look and snap photos of the colorful displays. The scents of fresh produce and flowers put everyone in a good mood and the atmosphere is friendly.

History

Cours Saleya was renovated in the late 1700s. Public terraces were built on the rooftops of the buildings lining the south side of the square, providing a place to stroll and enjoy sea views and sunsets.

The first wave of rich British tourists who came to spend their winters in Nice settled here, and Cours Saleya was lined with boutiques that appealed to them. They hosted elegant, illuminated garden parties and visited literary salons. They went to the opera and strolled along the terraces. Cours Saleya was the place to be seen!

In the late 1800s, the area started to become more workaday and less fashionable. The market was established here and Cours Saleya was losing its status as a place of culture. The new area of Nice, just across the Paillon River, was now the stylish quarter. The carnival, which had taken place in Cours Saleya for years, moved to the new area, and so did the shops that depended on the wealthy winter residents for their livelihood. Cours Saleya was deserted by the fickle aristocrats.

In 1900, the market in the center of Cours Saleya was covered with a metal structure. Then in the 1930s, it was replaced with a concrete one which was used as a parking garage when the market wasn't open. The terraces which had been left to deteriorate were closed to the public in the 1960s. Cours Saleya had lost its charm.

The fumes add a certain "je ne sais quoi" to the flavor

Thankfully, in the 1980s the concrete building was taken down and an underground parking facility was built. Cours Saleya was opened back up and made into a pedestrian area. It was, at last, able to regain its former character.

Flower Market

Today, Cours Saleya is known for its charming *Marché aux Fleurs*, or "Flower Market," held here Tuesday through Sunday mornings. It's actually a combination of the flower market and the fruit and vegetable market but the name, *Marché aux Fleurs* is commonly applied to the whole thing.

Maybe the flowers get special recognition because of their importance in Nice's history. In 1897 Nice opened the first wholesale cut flower market in the world. The growers in the hills would bring down their cut flowers every morning. After the wholesalers had made their bulk purchases, the market would be opened for individuals to buy their bouquets.

At that time, Nice was producing more flowers than all of Holland. Thanks to the railroads, carloads of these blooms were shipped to cities across France and Europe every day for almost 100 years.

One story says that Tsar Nicholas II of Russia was inspired by the flower parade he had seen in Nice and wanted to create a similar one in St. Petersburg. He ordered two train wagons full of flowers which sped across the rails and arrived in Russia a day and a half later.

Today, the wholesale section of the flower market has moved to another location but a group of flower sellers can still be found at the west end of Cours Saleya, supplying the daily floral needs of the Niçois.

The largest part of the market, however, is made up of colorful fruit and vegetables, often quite artistically displayed. The sellers tempt the passersby with samples. And it works, of course. After a taste of melt-in-your-mouth melon how could you resist taking one home for later? If you need ideas for how to prepare or serve an item, the vendors are happy to dispense that advice as well. Along with all the tantalizing fresh produce you can also find products such as spices, olives, honey, soaps, etc. You will always buy more than you had planned so be sure take an extra bag.

The only day you won't find flowers and food in Cours Saleya is Monday. That's the day for the *Marché à la Brocante*, the antiques/flea market. Here you can find all manner of items, such as furniture, jewelry, books, vintage clothing, bric-a-brac, etc. So, whether you are looking for flowers, produce, antiques, books, or art, you can surely find it in Cours Saleya.

Other Markets

♦ **Place du Palais de Justice** – Just one street behind Cours Saleya is the Place du Palais de Justice where there are markets almost every Saturday. The first, third, and fourth Saturdays of the month, you'll find a book market selling everything from used paperbacks to beautiful rare books. The second Saturday is a craft and painting market.

◆ **Place Saint François** – Another little market that might be worth a look is at the other end of the Old Town. It's the fish market at Place Saint François. It's small with just a few stands, but very popular with the seagulls who eagerly await the market's closing when they get to "clean up."

What to See

◆ **Sarde Palace** – Officially called the Préfecture Palace, this building isn't directly on Cours Saleya but is easily seen through the open square directly in front of it and beside the church. The building was built in the early 1600s as a palace for the Dukes of Savoy. Today it's home to the Préfet of the Alpes-Maritimes Department and is only occasionally open to the public.

◆ **Miséricorde Chapel, 7 Cours Saleya** – This church built in the 1700s is a gem of baroque architecture.

◆ **Matisse House, 1 Place Charles-Felix** – At one end of Cours Saleya stands a large yellow building where the artist Henri Matisse lived from 1921–1938. From his third-floor window he painted Cours Saleya and the sea. Later he moved up to the fourth floor for an even better view.

◆ **Terrace stairs** – The terraces are closed, but you can climb the stairs for an overview photo of the market.

◆ **Opera** – The opera house, built in 1885, is at the beginning of Cours Saleya, 4 Rue Saint François de Paule.

Fun Facts

♦ Carnival Parade – In 1830 the King and Queen of Sardinia were in Nice at carnival time. The city wanted to do something special and decided to have a parade. The King and Queen sat on the balcony of their palace (Sarde Palace) and watched the parade which went up and down Cours Saleya. The next year, when the king wasn't present, the people of Nice took some old clothes and some straw and made themselves a king to sit on the palace balcony and preside over the parade.

How Nice
Became French

In this chapter, when we speak of Nice, we are speaking of the historic County of Nice which covered the area roughly equivalent to what we today call the Department of the Alpes-Maritimes.

When you look around the old towns in this region, you will notice that the architecture has a distinct Italian flavor to it. Since this area is close to the Italian border and since it has only been part of France since 1860, you might reason that it must have been Italian before becoming French. But was it?

> *Italian?*
> *Never! ...*
> *Well, sort of...*

Italy became the country that we know and love today when most of the kingdoms, dukedoms, and republics scattered along the Italian peninsula united under King Victor-Emmanuel II. That process started in 1861 and since Nice became French the year before (in 1860), she never belonged to the modern state of Italy.

However, Nice was part of the House of Savoy, which became the Kingdom of Piedmont-Sardinia, which eventually became part of modern-day Italy. So even though Nice never belonged to the State of Italy, she did belong to a kingdom that became part of Italy (after she left). So technically, the answer is...

No, Nice was never part of Italy...
But in a way she was....

So now that we have clearly established Nice's relationship with Italy, let's discover how she became French. It all started way back in 1388...

Long-Term Relationship with Savoy

1388-1691

In 1388, Nice decided to join herself to the House of Savoy as a means of protection from the attacks of her unfriendly neighbor, Provence. This relationship between

Nice and Savoy was a long and happy one, lasting some 300 years.

It was during this association with Savoy that the French and Turkish armies united to attack the city of Nice in 1543. (Remember the famous battle in which Catherine Ségurane used her "secret weapon" to chase them away?) The invading armies succeeded in taking the town in spite of Catherine's bravery, but were unable to break through the defenses of the citadel on the hill. After sacking the lower town and learning that Savoy's allies were coming to Nice's aid, they decided to leave. So Nice was ravaged, but still with the House of Savoy.

Savoyard or French?

1691-1860

After Nice's long and stable relationship with the House of Savoy, she went through an identity crisis. She didn't know if she was Savoyard or French. Between 1691 and 1860 (169 years) Nice was shuffled back and forth between France and Savoy seven times. Each time it was the same scenario: France took her by force and then, after a number of years, she was given back to Savoy in a treaty.

It went something like this...

Starting in 1691
Nice was *French* for 6 years (1691-1697)
then *Savoyard* for 9 years (1697-1706)
then *French* for 7 years (1706-1713)
then *Savoyard* for 80 years (1713-1793)

then *French* for 21 years (1793-1814)
then *Sardinian* (because Savoy had become Piedmont-Sardinia) for 46 years (1814-1860)
then in 1860 Nice became *French* (*for good?*)

But there was something notably different about the changes in 1793 and 1860. The last two times the Niçois became French, they voted to to do so of their own free will.

Well, sort of...

First Vote to become French

1793

In 1793 France occupied Nice and intended to keep her. They started the process of the first official reattachment of Nice to France. They wanted a paper trail to prove they weren't annexing people against their will, so a public vote was held and the results were unanimously in favor of becoming French.

But only one-third of the cities and villages participated in the vote, which was closely supervised by French soldiers. Could that have had something to do with the outcome? It's difficult to say, but that was the first time the Niçois officially voted to become French.

Their happy days as baguette-munching French citizens lasted 21 years. Then when Napoleon I abdicated, the Treaty of Paris gave Nice back to the House of Savoy (which by that time had become Piedmont-Sardinia). So the Niçois turned in their baguettes and back they went. They stayed Sardinian for 46 years.

In 1859, the King of Sardinia (Victor-Emmanuel II) was looking to unite the states of the Italian peninsula and become king of the new country of Italy. When Austria threatened to spoil his plans, he went to his French neighbor for help. Napoleon III and Victor Emmanuel II signed a secret agreement. In exchange for France's help in fending off the Austrians, Nice would be given back to France. The deal was done, but there was just one little technicality. This change could only go into effect with the consent of the people.

Which brings us to the second vote...

Second Vote to become French

1860

When it was announced that there would be a vote on whether or not Nice would become French again, people divided into three camps. One group wanted to go with France, another wanted to stay with the King of Sardinia, and a third called for an independent state. It wasn't uncommon for fights to break out in the streets between opposing groups. They were taking their decision seriously.

But what those poor bruised brawlers didn't know was that their fate had already been decided. It would have been a huge embarrassment for both France and Sardinia if the vote did not match their previously signed agreement. So everyone did what they could to influence the people of Nice to vote "Yes for France."

Free...
With every "YES" vote

A massive "Vote Yes" campaign was launched. Victor-Emmanuel issued a proclamation releasing the people of Nice from their oath of loyalty to him and making them aware of the benefits of becoming a part of France. Napoleon sent in representatives to convince the Niçois of his good intentions while public officials and clergy did their best to persuade people to vote "Yes." The county was plastered with bulletins urging people to vote "Yes for France." Sardinian troops left and French troops arrived. All Sardinian administrative personnel were transferred out of Nice and replaced by Niçois. The message was pretty clear to everyone that they were becoming French even before the vote.

On the day, it was difficult to vote "no." The voting was presided over by French troops, there was no private voting booth, and just as a precaution, only "yes" ballots were supplied. Many who were against the annexation abstained from voting.

The result? Once again, Nice enthusiastically voted to become French – by 99% of the vote. Even if you count the abstentions, it would still have been 83% in favor of becoming French once again. The "Vote Yes" campaign had paid off. The Niçois happily picked up their baguettes, rejoined *La France* and haven't looked back since.

Well, sort of...

Immediately after the vote, Giuseppe Garibaldi, a Niçois politician and soldier who was against the annexation, claimed the vote was fixed. Even today, there is a small group that still maintains that the vote was illegal and they campaign for the independence of Nice. But for the most part, the people of Nice are content to munch their baguettes and be French.

What to See

♦ *Monument Centenaire* in the garden, Albert I – In 1893 this statue was erected for the 100-year anniversary of the first vote for the annexation of Nice. It was dated 1793–1893. (The 46 years during that time when Nice wasn't French were simply ignored.)

In 1960, when the 100-year anniversary of the second vote rolled around, they simply added the dates "1860–1960" under the other dates. And why not? They already had a perfectly good monument.

♦ *Neuf Lignes Obliques* ("Nine Oblique Lines") on the Promenade des Anglais – This sculpture by Bernar Venet was installed in 2010 for the 150th anniversary of the last annexation (1860). The nine lines represent the nine valleys which form the County of Nice.

♦ **Garibaldi Statue, Place Garibaldi** – Giuseppe Garibaldi was born Joseph Garibaldi in 1807 during a time when Nice was under French rule. However, from the age of seven onward, he was Sardinian (because Nice was given back to Sardinia). He was a politician and a general who played an active role in the creation of the modern state of Italy and he desperately wanted Nice to be a part of it.

However, before he took up the struggle for Italian unification, Garibaldi went all over the world helping those he saw as fighting for a worthy cause. He raised an "Italian Legion" of red-shirt-wearing soldiers that followed him from place to place. In Uruguay he participated in their civil war, and in Brazil, he took the part of the rebels of Rio Grande do Sul who wanted to separate from Brazil.

But when stirrings of the unification of Italy started, Garibaldi and his men headed back to join the fight. The states of Italy became unified, but to Garibaldi's bitter disappointment, Nice became French instead of Italian. Garibaldi claimed that the vote to become French was illegal, but eventually accepted the fact that his beloved city would remain French.

During the American Civil War (1861-1865), Garibaldi wrote offering his services to Abraham Lincoln. Garibaldi was offered a command but said he would only accept if the President declared that the motive of the war was to abolish slavery. At that time Lincoln wasn't ready to do that so Garibaldi stayed home.

PART 2: TRAIL OF TOURISM

At the end of the 1700s, the city of Nice was small and relatively poor. But then Tobias Smollett arrived. He was a Scottish writer and surgeon who wrote about his travels through France and Italy. In his book, he extolled the virtues of Nice's warm winter climate. At about the same time, another Scotsman, a doctor called John Brown, came up with the theory of "climate-therapy." He prescribed a change of climate for those suffering from certain conditions such as tuberculosis. He believed that breathing fresh, clean air could heal lung conditions – and sea air was the best air of all.

As a result of the efforts of these two Scotsmen, the French Riviera began to fill with rich, sickly British people. But as word spread about Nice's mild winter climate, other healthier aristocrats started to arrive as well. Of course, they weren't all British, there were Russians, Germans, Belgians, and others, but because of the abundance of British, the word "English" became synonymous with "tourist."

Alexandre Dumas wrote in 1851, that "for the inhabitants of Nice, all tourists are English. Every foreigner, regardless of appearance, comes from a strange city lost in the fog, where they have only heard stories about the sun, where they have never seen oranges or pineapples, where the only ripe fruits they have are cooked apples, and they call that city London."

Another time, when Alexandre Dumas checked into a hotel in Nice, he asked the clerk about the nationality of the people who had just checked in before him. The clerk answered, "They are English, but I don't know if they are French or German." (Remember, at that time Nice wasn't yet French.)

The first British winter tourists stayed in the Old Town, near the opera. As more and more long-stay tourists arrived, some of them moved to the hills surrounding Nice. Others started communities across the Paillon River, in what has become the new area of Nice. Every year, there were more foreign winter visitors: In 1861 there were 4,500; in 1881 there were 33,000; and in 1910 there were 150,000. Some even jokingly referred to Nice as a British colony.

The aristocrats had discovered Nice in the late 1700s, but it wasn't until the mid 1860s that the royals started to appear. In 1865 the railway reached Nice and paved the way for royals from throughout Europe to arrive in their private trains with cars full of servants, and household furnishing. Kings and queens wintered in Nice, including Queen Victoria of Great Britain and the Russian Tsarinas.

All these aristocratic and royal visitors boosted the economy and were responsible for many changes in Nice. Then in the 1920s, the Americans arrived and changed things even more. But we'll read about that in the following chapters.

Queen Victoria

CRND

A Queen and her Donkey

Of all the rich and royal visitors to Nice in the 1800s, one of the most famous and the best-loved by the Niçois was Queen Victoria of Great Britain. While vacationing on the French Riviera, she would leave her crown on the shelf and go by the less conspicuous name of "Lady Balmoral." Perhaps this was in an effort to keep a low profile.

When the Queen (I mean Lady Balmoral) began to visit Nice, she was 76 years old, short, round, and always dressed in black. She would arrive in her own special train, accompanied by nearly one hundred staff members. These included bagpipe-playing Scottish soldiers dressed in kilts, and turban-wearing Indian soldiers. (So much for keeping a low profile.)

Her train carried wagonloads of luggage, not counting the Queen's bed and other furniture which arrived ahead of her and was already set up in the eighty-odd rooms she rented in the Excelsior Regina Palace, the luxury hotel in the hills of Cimiez that had been built specifically with her in mind. The building sports a crown atop the west wing which the Queen occupied on her winter visits.

Also sent in advance were her carriages, horses and a donkey... yes, a donkey. Jacquot (pronounced Jacko) was the donkey the Queen had bought on one of her holidays in Provence. She had trouble walking and was frustrated because her carriage was too large to take her down the many intriguing alleyways she wanted to explore.

When she saw a peasant with a small cart pulled by a handsome but underfed donkey, she stopped and asked the man how much he had paid for the poor beast. When he responded, "100 francs," the Queen said, "I will give you 200." The deal was done, and traveling behind Jacquot in her little donkey cart became the favorite mode of transportation of the ruler of one quarter of the world.

We can imagine that Jacquot was well fed and lived a life of luxury from then on. He traveled back and forth between England and France with the Queen and even to other European destinations.

When in Nice, Victoria kept to her strict daily schedule. She would start with a full English breakfast, with musical accompaniment, in the hotel garden, weather permitting. After a few hours of paperwork, the Sovereign of the empire on which the sun never set would climb into her little donkey cart and tootle around the gardens of Cimiez behind Jacquot. After the garden visits, queen and donkey would return to the hotel for lunch.

After lunch, Queen Victoria would venture out further in a larger carriage pulled by horses. She would meander through the hills and along the coast, visiting interesting sites and towns in the area. Sometimes she would stop in a local restaurant for tea. But it wasn't the restaurant staff that made the tea for the Queen. No, Victoria traveled with all the necessary tea-making supplies and the staff to brew her a proper cuppa. She wasn't taking any chances, as the French aren't known for their tea-making skills.

She would stop to watch games of boules (similar to lawn bowling), attend the gourd festival, the carnival (where she reportedly threw flowers at handsome young soldiers), and any other local festivity she happened upon. She exhibited a curiosity about everything that she encountered. It was that curiosity and interest in the local culture that endeared her to the Niçois.

Victoria had wintered in other areas along the Riviera, but once she discovered Nice she kept returning. She spent five successive winters in Nice, from 1895–1899. The following winter she had to forgo her Nice holiday because of the controversy surrounding the British actions in the Boer Wars. Then the next year, in 1901, while wintering on the Isle of Wight she took ill and died. It's reported that she said, "If only I were in Nice, I would get better."

The Queen is commemorated in Nice with a statue in front of the Hotel Regina-Excelsior in Cimiez where she stayed. There is also "Avenue Reine Victoria" named for her in the area where she used to ride in her donkey cart in Cimiez.

What to See

♦ **Excelsior Regina Palace,** 71 Boulevard Cimiez – This grand building was built as a hotel mostly for Queen Victoria. The west wing, where she would take eighty or so rooms each winter, is topped by a crown. In the 1930s the hotel was converted into apartments and is no longer open to the public.

♦ **Statue of Queen Victoria** – This statue sits downhill in front of the Excelsior Regina Palace where the Queen used to stay. After her death in 1901, a local newspaper, Le Petit Niçois, raised funds from the people of Nice for the monument. The British Queen was beloved by the Niçois for her generosity, her curious spirit, and because she took an interest in Nice and its people.

The statue was erected in 1912 and depicts Victoria receiving bouquets of flowers from four young girls. The four girls represent the four cities where she had stayed: Nice, Cannes, Grasse, and Menton. This statue has been granted historic monument status.

♦ **Stationer to the Queen**, 5 Rue Alexandre Mari, in the Old Town – On the side of this stationery shop is a sign saying "By Appointment Stationer to H. M. the Queen Victoria."

Fun Facts

♦ **Jacquot** – Some sources say that Jacquot finished out his days at Windsor Castle. But the Niçois say that for many years after he died, the stuffed Jacquot stood at the entrance of the Museum of Natural History in Nice. Whether it was really Jacquot or another donkey standing in for him, we can't say. But we do know that in the early 1970s, the museum donkey had an unfortunate weevil infestation and had to be destroyed.

Promenade des Anglais

❦

A Very English Idea

One of the main attractions to be found in Nice is the *Promenade des Anglais*, that ribbon of activity that follows the curve of the bay through Nice. It's a place for all to mix and mingle. On the wide pedestrian thoroughfare you can see people walking, jogging, skating, and biking. Those less sporty among us can just sit and enjoy the view, either of the calming blue waves or of the sunbathers on the pebbly beach below.

But you might be wondering about the name. Promenade des Anglais means "Avenue of the English." So what is an English avenue doing in this French city? Well, to find out, we have to go back to the early 1800s, to the time when many wealthy English tourists were coming to spend their winters in Nice. Those vacationing Victorians developed their own little colony in the area to the west of the Old Town, where they built villas, hotels, and their own Anglican church and cemetery. At that time, this area was rural and situated outside the city.

Since many of these winter visitors had come to the area to regain their failing health, they wanted to be able to walk or ride in their carriages along the sea and breathe in the health-restoring sea air. But there was a problem. The seafront was an impassable, rocky marsh that kept them from reaping all the benefits of the area.

At the same time that these church-going, sun-seeking English visitors were dreaming of walking by the sea, another problem arose. The region was hit by hard times. Two seasons of bad harvests reduced many people in Nice to begging. And where did they go to ask for money? To the rich tourists, of course. But giving charity to those physically able to work was contrary to the early nineteenth-century British mindset. They believed it demoralized the poor and led to dependence on handouts.

Luckily, the Anglican priest, Reverend Lewis Way came up with a brilliant plan. He saw the opportunity to remedy the situation of both the English and the Niçois with one project. He took up a collection among the English to build their longed-for seaside promenade. Then he hired the down-on-their-luck Niçois to build it. It was a win-win situation. The English would have their healthy walks by the sea and the poor would find honorable work.

In 1824 the first promenade was completed and the ailing English could walk by the sea. The modest unpaved road was six feet (two meters) wide. Officially it was called the *strada del littorale*, or "seaside road," but the people of Nice called it *camin dei Inglés* which in French became the *Promenade des Anglais* (English Promenade) because it was financed by and built for the use of the English community.

In 1835, the city took over the upkeep of the "Prom" and it has been enlarged and improved many times over the years. The result is what we see today, a wide boulevard with lanes for pedestrians, bikes, and automobiles, running along the magnificent azure sea. It's a wonderful example of something beautiful being created by people working together to solve their problems. Well done, Victorians!

What to See

♦ **Anglican Church,** 11 Rue de la Buffa – Construction started on the present neo-gothic style church building in 1860, but there has been an Anglican church on the site since the 1820s. This British settlement in the countryside was known as Newborough for many years.

The first Anglican church on the site was built in the style of a house because in the Kingdom of Sardinia, to which Nice belonged at the time, only Roman Catholic churches were built. Special permission had to be granted for others and they could not resemble churches. When the present building was started, however, Nice was part of France and the restrictions on church buildings had been lifted.

One thing to note is the coat of arms over the entrance (on the inside). It used to be in Queen Victoria's private chapel in the Excelsior Regina Palace hotel where she would take up residence in the winter. The quaint little church cemetery was used from 1820 to 1860.

♦ **Architecture along the Prom** – At one time the Promenade was lined with beautiful belle époque buildings. Unfortunately, many were destroyed and replaced by what you see today. There are, however, still a few buildings worth a look.

-**Palais de la Méditerrané** – This hotel and casino was funded by Frank J. Gould, an American businessman, in 1929. All that's left of the original building is the facade which narrowly escaped destruction by being designated a historic monument in 1989.

-Villa Massena, 35 Promenade des Anglais and 65 Rue de France (entrance) – This former villa is now a museum of the history of Nice. It was built as a winter residence for a wealthy Parisian at the end of the nineteenth century.

-Negresco – A symbol of Nice, this hotel opened in 1913. It was built for Henri Negresco, a Romanian immigrant who came to France without a penny. He worked his way up, becoming a master chef, and then succeeded in convincing two wealthy businessmen to finance his hotel venture.

♦ Blue chairs (chaises bleues) – The blue chairs on the Promenade have become one of the symbols of Nice. They first appeared in 1950, and at that time, you had to pay to sit. Ticket-sellers patrolled the Prom insuring that no one sat without paying. Originally, individual chairs were set out, but they had to be connected together to prevent them from being taken as souvenirs. There's a large blue chair sculpture on the Prom and you will see other references throughout the city to this Niçois icon.

Fun Facts

♦ *Quai des Etats-Unis* (Quay of the United States) – England isn't the only country to be honored along the seafront. The extension of the Promenade des Anglais just across from the Old Town is called the Quay of the United States. It was given this name in 1917 in honor of the United States' decision to enter World War I on the side of the Allies.

Noontime Cannon

How a Scottish Lord Got his Wife's Attention

Visitors to Nice are often startled by a very loud noontime boom. It occurs every day at precisely 12:00 and is a remnant from the Victorian times, when a British wife just couldn't remember to go home for lunch.

It was 1861, it was lunchtime, and Thomas Coventry-More was hungry. This Scottish Lord (let's call him Tom) and his wife were spending their winter in Nice, as usual, and the missus was late coming home for lunch, as usual. Every morning she would go out for a stroll, meet other British ladies, and spend hours gossiping about who was doing what on the French Riviera. She often forgot all about having lunch with her poor husband who was sitting at home alone waiting for her.

Tom was an ex-British army officer and a punctual man. He wanted to eat lunch at the specified hour and not one minute later. But he was also a problem-solver, so he set out to solve this one. He thought about his army experiences and in no time at all, he had a plan. A perfectly simple plan. He went to see the Nice City Council, since he needed their cooperation, and explained his idea.

To make sure they had understood his Scottish accent, they repeated his proposition.

"You want us to go to the top of the hill everyday at noon and shoot off a cannon, which will surely frighten our citizens, just to remind your wife to come home for lunch?"

"Yes, that's it, old chap, you've understood perfectly. Of course, since it's mainly for my benefit, I'll pay all of the costs and I even have an old cannon lying around that I will donate for the task."

The council huddled together to make their decision.

"These English are crazy!" (To the French all British are English – even if they are Scottish.)

"Yes, he is crazy, but he is going to pay..."

"It will frighten people at first, but then the Niçois will get used to it, and it will only frighten the tourists – that could be fun."

"Well, yes, why not?" And Tom's plan was approved.

"Wonderful!" Exclaimed Tom, "I'll arrange everything and we'll start next week. Have your man up on the hill by 11.45. I'll go to the roof of my hotel and hoist a colored ball up a pole to signal when it's noon. The cannon will be fired at twelve noon *precisely*."

All went along very well like this for years, until finally, Tom and his wife stopped coming to Nice. Since he was no longer paying the expenses, the council stopped firing the cannon. Havoc ensued in Nice! People were late for lunch or even worse, missed it altogether – all because there was no cannon boom to remind them when to eat.

Well, this was just not acceptable and the council had to reinstate the noonday signal. Of course, today it's no longer a cannon that we hear, but a firework. It's still set off manually each day at noon and now the Niçois never miss their lunch. Even if they've grown so used to the midday boom that they hardly notice it, they know it's lunchtime when all the tourists jump.

What to See

♦ You can't see the firework being shot off from the *Colline du Château* (Castle Hill). The location is closed to the public for security reasons. You might be able to see a little cloud of smoke from the firework explosion if you look very carefully.

Fun Facts

♦ Every year on April 1, the firework is set off one hour early as an April Fool's joke.

Castle Hill

Finding the Castle is a Walk in the Park

If you like looking at castles and chateaux, you'll probably want to go up to the *Colline du Château*, or "Castle Hill" to see Nice's castle. But no matter how hard you look, you won't find it.

You'll see some gorgeous views, a waterfall, some archeological ruins of a fifth-century church, a lovely park... but where is that famous castle? You would think a castle should be easy to find, but it's nowhere to be seen. As it turns out there hasn't been a castle on this hill for more than 300 years. But the hill is still referred to as *la Colline du Château*, and the hilltop simply as le *Château*, or "the Castle."

Even though there's no castle (just a few ruins remain) it's a beautiful park with stunning views over Nice and the *Baie des Anges*. The few hundred stairs up to the top of the hill aren't too difficult because there are lots of places to stop, catch your breath and admire the view along the way. But if the stairs are too much for you, there is an elevator in the tower, or you can take the little tourist train to the top. There are also several roads from the Old Town – any one going uphill will do.

This hilltop was where the Greeks settled around the fourth century BC. It was their acropolis of Nikaia. But the few bits of castle that remain are from a much later era. They are from a tenth-century castle that stood on this hill for about 700 years. It was enlarged over the centuries and became a fortified city which spilled down into the area that

Where's the castle everyone is talking about?

is today the Old Town of Nice. The whole area – the castle on the hill as well as the town below – was surrounded by protective walls. At the end of the seventeenth century, Nice was one of the most fortified cities in Europe.

This walled castle that had warded off invaders for hundreds of years was considered impregnable until Louis XIV came along in the early 1700s. His army bombarded the castle and walls with thousands of cannonballs and the King's brand new weapon, the incendiary bomb. The old castle finally fell, and to teach the Niçois a lesson, King Louis had the entire castle razed to the ground. At the same time, all the walls surrounding the castle and the town below were destroyed.

With Nice's protective walls gone, it was left open to another invasion – this time a much less violent one. In the late 1700s the English started to trickle in, but by the mid 1800s it must have seemed to the people of Nice like a full-blown British invasion. Victorians were everywhere. And what did these Victorians like to do? They liked to take walks – by the seaside, in nature, anywhere they could breathe in the fresh air that they thought would cure their ills.

In 1820, the King of Sardinia (because Nice was once again Sardinian) wanted to encourage this new tourism. He gave the *Colline du Château* to the city on the condition that it be made into a botanical garden and park. It was designed in the romantic style that was popular among the Victorian visitors. The old castle tower was rebuilt and a man-made waterfall was installed to add the charming, romantic touches the English adored. The mosaics with Greek motifs are a 1960s addition.

Remember the Victorian midday cannon? It was fired from one of the terraces of the "castle." It's amusing that the midday boom, which reminds the Niçois that it's lunchtime, is still referred to as the *canon du château*, or "cannon of the castle," when in fact, there is neither a cannon nor a castle. But you have to admit that the "cannon of the castle" is more romantic than the "firework of the hilltop."

What to See

♦ **Views** – From the hilltop, you will have beautiful views of the *Baie des Anges* and the port of Nice. Sunrises and sunsets are especially stunning from this vantage point.

♦ **Waterfall** – A big manmade waterfall cascading over fake ruins was just what was needed to complete the romantic atmosphere of the park. The water arrives by way of a canal that comes from the Vesubie River. The canal and waterfall were built in the late 1800s.

♦ **Mosaics** – The Greek motif mosaics were installed by the City of Nice in the 1960s as a nod to its Greek heritage. Of special note are stairs depicting the story of Homer's Odyssey. There are a few matching mosaics in the garden, Albert I.

Fun Facts

♦ **Napoleon III** – In 1860 just after Nice became French again, Emperor Napoleon III visited the park and declared it the most beautiful landscape he had ever seen.

♦ **Germans** – During the occupation of 1943–1944 the Germans installed cannons on the hill where they would have a clear shot at any approaching ships. They also tunneled into the rock to create barracks and passageways leading from the beach to the hilltop. One such passageway was fitted with an iron spiral staircase stripped out of the Jetée Promenade Casino, a casino inspired by London's Crystal Palace and destroyed by the Germans.

♦ **Elevator** – The elevator that takes visitors to the top of the hill today is inside a huge well shaft that was dug down through the rock in the 1500s.

♦ **The Garden Albert I** (next to Casino Ruhl) was also built around the same time as the park on the hill – both with the Victorians in mind.

Three Tsarinas Leave Their Mark

Russian Monuments in Nice

The British weren't the only aristocrats to take advantage of Nice's warm winters. There has been a strong Russian community here since the mid 1800s when Russian nobles would spend their winters mingling with the rest of Europe's high society. The Tsars tended to stay home and run the country, but the more delicate Tsarinas preferred to pass their winters in the Riviera sunshine. In Nice, a church, a chapel, and a cathedral remind us of three generations of Tsarinas who made this their winter home.

Tsarina No. 1
and the First Russian Church

Alexandra Feodorovna (1798-1860)
Wife of Tsar Nicholas I and
mother of Tsar Alexander II

In 1856, when Alexandra was 48 years old and widowed, she became the first Tsarina to winter in the French Riviera. She came for her health, but there was also another reason. Her son, the Tsar, sent her to sweet-talk the King of Sardinia and strengthen the bond between the two powers. (At that time, Nice was in the Kingdom of Sardinia). She was accompanied by her other son, who was commander of the Russian Navy.

While Alexandra was charming the King, her son negotiated an agreement to allow Russian ships to dock in the port of Villefranche-sur-Mer, just down the coast from Nice. Russia had lost access to the Black Sea in the Crimean War and needed a place to park their ships. For Sardinia, the Russian fleet was protection against Austria, who liked to invade them from time to time. So a deal was made and a Russian naval presence was established in Villefranche that lasted until 1870.

After Alexandra's successful meetings with the King in Genoa, she took a ship to Villefranche where she was welcomed by crowds of cheering locals. Then she headed to Nice to start her winter holiday. Once settled in, she was presented with a project: the Russian Orthodox community wanted a church, but the state religion of Piedmont-

Sardinia was Roman Catholicism and only Roman Catholic churches could be built.

Dearest King of Sardinia,
Thank you the boat thing.
I have just one more little
favor to ask. We would like
your permission to build a
Russian Orthodox Church
in Nice.
Your friend,
Alexandra,
*   Mother of the Tsar*

However, two years earlier, the English had been given special permission to build an Anglican church, so the Russians decided to make their request too. The local authorities, afraid of a negative community reaction, dragged their feet. Finally, the two governments (St. Petersburg and Turin) stepped in and permission was granted by royal decree.

The local authorities agreed but only under certain conditions: the church was not to look like a church, it was to blend with the surrounding buildings, and no bells were allowed. This is why the ground floor of this building houses a library and the sanctuary is discretely tucked away upstairs. The architect did, however, sneak in a little surprise – a dome which wasn't on the plans. It can only be seen from a distance, but it was shocking to many locals.

This church was built between 1858 and 1859 and named the Church of St. Nicholas and St. Alexandra to honor the Tsarina who was influential in its construction and her deceased husband, Nicholas I. It's located at 6 Rue Longchamp.

Tsarina No. 2
and the Chapel Tzarewitch

Maria Alexandrovna (1824-1880)
Wife of Alexander II and
daughter-in-law to Tsarina No. 1

Our second Tsarina, Maria, was the daughter-in-law of Alexandra, the first Tsarina to come to Nice. She continued the tsarina tradition of spending winters on the French Riviera, but her legacy to Nice is a sad one. In the winter of 1865 her son, Nicholas Alexandrovitch, came to Nice to visit her. The 21-year-old Tsarevich, "son of the Tsar" was next in line for the throne but sadly, while he was here, an old injury worsened and he became gravely ill. As he lay dying, the people of Nice stood outside the building in silence, mourning with the Imperial Family.

His grief-stricken parents bought the grounds and villa in which the Tsarevich died. They tore down the villa, and built a chapel in the exact location where his deathbed had been. It's a memorial chapel, as the body was sent back to Russia for burial. This chapel is located behind the Russian Orthodox Cathedral on Avenue Nicolas II, just off Boulevard du Tzarewitch.

Tsarina No. 3
and the Russian Cathedral

Maria Feodorovna (1847-1928)
Wife of Alexander III and
daughter-in-law of Tsarina No. 2

Maria was originally engaged to Nicolas Alexandrovitch (the young Tsarevich who died in Nice). But she ended up marrying his brother who became Tsar Alexander III. About thirty years later (in 1896), Maria was a 49-year-old widow wintering in the Nice sunshine when she learned of plans to build a new Russian Orthodox church to replace the  one on Longchamp which had become too small for the growing congregation. She took the project to heart and convinced her son, Nicholas II to pay for most of it out of his own pocket.

This time, there were no restrictions to keep the Russians from building a proper church. Nice had become a part of France and embraced religious freedom, so the Russian community could have their Russian-style cathedral –

bells and all. The exuberant building that resulted represented Russia in all her glory.

At first, the plan had been to raze the church on Longchamp and replace it with the new cathedral, but the site was too small. Next they chose a site at the corner of Rues Verdi and Berlios. Unfortunately, the soil there wasn't suitable for such a large structure. So Maria asked her son, Tsar Nicholas II, to donate some of the land next to the Tsarevich chapel and that turned out to be the perfect spot.

The architect had designed a beautiful building for the previous corner lot which had two large identical entrances to take advantage of access from both streets. Even though the new location wasn't on a corner, the architect decided to keep the design. That's why today you find two entrances to the cathedral, only one of which is used.

The first stone was laid in 1903 and the building was finished in 1912. Today, it sits like a little jewel, in a green park on Avenue Nicolas II, just off Boulevard du Tzarewitch.

These three monuments, which are tied to the history of these Tsarinas, are still used and enjoyed by the Russian community in Nice today.

What to See

♦ **Russian Church** – 6 Rue Longchamp.

♦ **Chapel** – Avenue Nicolas II, just behind the cathedral.

♦ **Cathedral** – Avenue Nicolas II, off Boulevard du Tzare-witch.

♦ **Lycée du Parc Imperial**, 2 Avenue Suzanne Lenglen – This school building, which sits up the hill from the cathedral, was originally a luxury hotel, Hotel Parc Imperial for the Russian aristocracy. It was built in 1902 and the City acquired it in 1925.

♦ **Russian Cemetery**, 7 Place Caucade (outside city center) – In 1867 a parcel of land was purchased by Russia on Caucade Hill to be used as a Russian cemetery. There is also an English cemetery and a military cemetery next to it.

Fun Facts

♦ *Basse Corniche* – It's thanks to Tsarina No. 1, Alexandra Feodorovna, that we have a nice smooth road between Nice and Villefranche. She would arrive by ship to the port of Villefranche and make her way to Nice by carriage. It seems the ride was just too bumpy for the Tsarina so she donated the funds to have it smoothed. Work on the *Basse Corniche* started in 1857 and the Tsarina was the guest of honor at the inauguration ceremony.

♦ **Size Matters** – The cathedral in Nice is the largest Russian Orthodox cathedral outside Russia.

♦ **Who owns the cathedral?** The cathedral was at the center of a court battle from 2007 to 2013. The land had been owned by the tsars since the mid 1860s, when Nicholas II gave a 99-year lease to the Archbishop of St. Petersburg to build and operate a cathedral on it. But in 1917, with the Russian Revolution, Russia lost interest in maintaining this faraway building. A local cultural organization, ACOR, was formed in 1923 to maintain the cathedral and manage the day-to-day affairs.

In 2007 the lease expired and Russia wanted their cathedral back, but ACOR didn't want to give it up. They claimed their 80-plus years of care entitled them to the building. The court in Nice ruled in Russia's favor, and ACOR appealed. The court in Aix-en-Provence upheld the first decision and ACOR appealed. That appeal was denied and the property belongs to the Russian Federation which is successor to the Tsars.

♦ **A Russian Naval Base** operated in Villefranche-sur-Mer from 1858-1870.

♦ **Russian Immigration** – The first Russians were aristocrats who came to pass their winters in Nice. Then in 1917, a wave of Russian immigrants arrived to flee the Bolshevik Revolution.

American Trendsetters

Who Wants to Swim in the Sea?

If you visit the French Riviera in July or August, you might have trouble finding an open space on the beach to put your towel. It's hard to imagine, but before 1920, there were no summer tourists here, no hotels were open, and there was certainly no one swimming in the sea.

The French Riviera was "discovered" in the 1800s by the European nobility who spent their winters here. But when springtime rolled around those wealthy vacationers headed home and left the locals to sizzle under the summer sun. In the 1920s, however, that all changed thanks to an American couple who "rediscovered" the Riviera.

The Murphys

Gerald and Sara Murphy were wealthy Americans who, along with many other artistic souls, left the US for Europe in the early 1920s. One reason for this exodus was that the postwar atmosphere had become stifling there. The Eighteenth Amendment had passed and prohibition made it illegal to produce, transport, or sell alcoholic beverages. Overnight, thousands of law-abiding citizens were reclassified as criminals. Crime rose and criminal organizations gained strength.

The Murphys and many others took advantage of the strong US dollar and went to live in Europe. When they arrived in Paris with their three young children and a nanny, they were captivated by the creative energy there. In Europe where every home had lost someone to the war, the young people wanted to forget about death and destruction. They just wanted to live and celebrate. This was the beginning of *Les Années Folles*, or the "Crazy Years" in which creativity boomed. Modernism was born and Paris became the center of all things artistic. There, you could find painters, writers, and musicians from around the world forging new forms of their art.

Gerald's first glimpse of modern art had a profound effect on him. He decided then and there to start painting. Both he and Sara took lessons and while Sara eventually quit, Gerald went on to become a somewhat admired painter. Even though his career was short, he produced some impressive works.

While in Paris, the Murphys put their newly-learned painting skills into practice and donated their time to help restore the backdrops for the Russian ballet which had been destroyed in a fire. There they met other artists, including Pablo Picasso, and found their niche in the artistic community. Many of the modern artists living in Paris were young and wild, but Gerald and Sara were a bit older and had three children. They enjoyed the creative synergy of the art scene but led a settled life and were known as masters of the art of living well.

Discovering the Riviera

In the summer of 1922 the Murphys came to the South of France to visit Cole Porter, one of Gerald's friends from Yale. Cole, who had a reputation for finding charming and unusual holiday destinations, had rented a villa in Antibes. That was the only summer Cole ever spent in the area, but the Murphys fell in love with the Riviera and knew immediately that was where they wanted to live.

The next summer the Murphys returned. Normally, all the hotels closed on May 1 because this was a place for winter holidays. There were no tourists in the summer. Gerald and Sara convinced the owner of the Hotel du Cap in Antibes to stay open for them, and that summer they entertained the first of their many visitors who would come from Paris, Pablo Picasso and his family. Picasso also fell in love with the area and rented a villa in Antibes.

Gerald and Sara bought a place just below the Antibes lighthouse. It had a magnificent garden but the villa

required two years of renovation. Always trendsetters, the Murphys added features to their home that were unheard of at the time, such as a flat roof that could be used as a terrace. The interior was very modern with black floors and white walls, mirrors and stainless steel. They moved in with their three children in the summer of 1924 and called their new home Villa America.

The Murphys made monthly visits to Paris to stay in touch with the artistic community there, and they entertained a constant stream of their Parisian friends at Villa America. Their unusual behavior bewildered the locals and gave them something to gossip about.

Gerald cleared a layer of seaweed 4 ft. (1.20 meters) thick from the beach'to make a place for swimming. These strange Americans lay in the sun, swam in the sea, and picnicked in the sand while listening to jazz on a portable phonograph. Such shocking activities had never before been seen on the Riviera.

Some of the Murphys' friends, like Picasso and F. Scott Fitzgerald, followed in their footsteps and took up residence in the South of France. Others from the Paris arts scene started spending summer holidays here. Hotels began to stay open in summer to accommodate these guests and beaches were cleared of seaweed and began to fill with sunbathers. Summer on the Riviera would never be the same!

But, all good things must come to an end, and *Les Années Folles* ended abruptly in 1929 when the stock market crashed. The same year, one of Gerald and Sara's sons was diagnosed with tuberculosis and they left Europe for good in 1933 to go back to the US. But they had left their mark on the French Riviera and it had changed forever.

It's reported that as Picasso sat looking out over a beach that had been abandoned when the Murphys arrived and was now filled with sunbathers, he remarked that he and the Murphys had a lot to answer for. I wonder what he would think today.

Fun Facts

♦ **Famous Friends** – A list of Gerald and Sara's friends reads like a Who's Who of the 1920s. They rubbed shoulders with Cole Porter, Gertrude Stein, F. Scott Fitzgerald, Ernest Hemingway, John Dos Passos, Pablo Picasso, Rudolph Valentino, Jean Cocteau, Ezra Pound, Igor Stravinsky, and Fernand Léger among others.

♦ **Isadora Duncan** was one of the Americans who began to frequent the Riviera in the 1920s. She was a dancer known for her improvisational style and considered by some as the creator of modern dance. She was killed on the Promenade des Anglais when her very long flowing scarf became entangled in the wheel of the car she was riding in and strangled her. This happened just in front of the Negresco Hotel in 1927.

♦ **Josephine Baker** performed at the Palais de la Méditeranée in the 1920s and brought a little pig, wearing a pink ribbon, as her traveling companion. The staff of the hotel had to take it for walks on the Promenade.

♦ **Books by F. Scott Fitzgerald** – Fitzgerald and his wife, Zelda, came to live near the Murphys in 1924. He was greatly inspired and influenced by them and their Riviera lifestyle.
–**Tender is the Night** – in this book, dedicated to the Murphys, Fitzgerald's characters are a combination of the Murphys' personalities and lifestyle and his own.
–**The Great Gatsby** – This novel is set in the 1920s in the US, but much of it was written while Fitzgerald was in Antibes with the Murphys.

♦ **Rocky Beaches** – You might wonder why the beaches of Nice, with a few exceptions, are covered in pebbles. They're not at all comfortable to lie on or walk on, but that doesn't seem to stop people waddling like ducks out to the sea. Each year the City of Nice spends around 600,000 euros on rocks to replace those washed away every winter by the waves. For at least thirty years, the City has discussed changing over to sand, but it all comes down to cost. While sand is cheaper, it also washes away much more quickly and would require a special retention system to keep it in place. The last study, which was done around 2003, found that it would, indeed, be possible... at a cost of eighteen million euros... per kilometer. Better buy some plastic shoes and a thick mat.

PART 3:
DISASTER AND
DASTARDLY
DEEDS

In Nice, like everywhere else in the world, life isn't always rosy – crime and disaster are also a part of the history of this city. In this section we discover stories ranging from the rather mild defacing of a statue to horrible murders. So hold on to your hat!

Bank Robbers

Fire

War Crimes

Murder

Statue Defacing Hangings

Mafia Crime
Earthquake

Kidnapping

Dastardly Deeds

Disaster

Nice Opera

From Tragedy to Triumph

Like the mythological phoenix, the nineteenth-century opera house in the Old Town rose from the ashes of its predecessor. Then after a rather shaky start, it soared to success.

If you ask the locals about their lovely opera house, some of them might do a bit of name-dropping and tell you it was built by the famous French architect, Charles Garnier, who is known for the Paris opera house that bears his name. But in fact, it was the not-so-famous François Aune, official architect of the city of Nice, who designed it. His plans were then approved by the famous Charles Garnier, but only because Garnier happened to be the Inspector of Public Buildings at the time and it was his job to approve the plans of all civic structures being built in France. The local architect was, however, a student of Gustave Eiffel (there's another name to drop).

Thanks to techniques learned from Mr. Eiffel, the internal structure of the building makes use of iron beams for structural support – a thoroughly modern innovation at the time. The exterior, however, looks completely traditional with its pink stone facade being watched over by four statues representing the muses of Music, Tragedy, Comedy, and Dance. Inside, all is crimson opulence and splendor. Three levels of luxury boxes line the sides and one large royal box occupies the back. Mythological figures populate the frescoed ceiling while the large central chandelier represents the sun.

Even though this opera house was built in 1885, the location has a long history of entertainment. In 1776 the Marquise Alli-Maccarani turned her house, which stood on this site, into a small theater. There were several theaters in the area at this time because the wealthy British tourists had started to appear for the winter and they required entertainment. The theater was later enlarged and a royal box was added for the occasional royal visitor.

The atmosphere inside the theater, however, wasn't always conducive to enjoying the show. In 1793, the mayor banned smoking during the performances because, not only was it off-putting to those who weren't used to the smell, it was also a fire hazard. But the main reason for making the theater a smoke-free zone was because those seated in the back or in the boxes were not able to see the actors through the thick cloud of smoke hanging over the auditorium.

First Opera House

In 1826, the City of Nice wanted to rise a step above regular theater, and introduce opera which was considered more sophisticated. They bought the theater, tore it down, and built a large, proper Italian-style opera house in the same location. When it opened two years later, it was grand and luxurious. The huge curtain which closed off the stage was painted with a scene showing the heroic deeds of Catherine Ségurane. (Remember the Niçoise laundress who chased away the Turkish troops?) At the back of the stage was a huge window looking out over the sea. There were four levels of public boxes and a large royal box. It was called the Royal Theater, and it was sumptuous and elegant. But the elegance didn't make up for performances that were sometimes lackluster.

The poor-quality performances caused the people of Nice to lose their taste for opera. Attendance was so low that the Opera was turned into a regular theater (no singing) for five years.

In 1833, the city made an attempt to reintroduce opera. An orchestra was hired and opera performances recommenced. But in 1857, the newspaper reported that on one particular evening, the conductor was so bad the musicians went to sleep during the performance.

But sprinkled among the snore-worthy performances, there must have been some more inspired evenings because the opera continued and developed a clientele of kings, rich tourists, and Niçois and became an integral part of life in Nice.

The opera house was a place of celebration in 1860 when Nice became French. A special opera was written for the occasion called, *Nice Française*. It was free and open to everyone. But becoming a part of France under the Emperor Napoleon III meant that the name of the opera house had to be changed from *Royal Theater* to *Imperial Theater*. Speaking of the Emperor, in 1860 he and the Empress Eugenie opened a ball at the Nice opera house with Johan Strauss leading the orchestra. I don't imagine the musicians were falling asleep that evening.

When France became a republic again in 1870, the opera house's name was changed once more. This time it became the *Municipal Theater*. With so many wealthy, pleasure-seeking visitors, the building was put to good use. As well as opera and theater productions, sometimes the seating area would be turned into a dance floor covered with flowers and the orchestra would be set up on the stage.

But tragedy struck on March 23, 1881. At the beginning of a performance, there was a gas explosion from one of the footlights. The curtain burst into flames and the fire spread quickly throughout the building. The lights went out, leaving hundreds of panicking people scrambling to escape in the dark. The exits were insufficient and around sixty people died in the devastating fire. The church across the street was filled with cadavers and five funeral carriages draped in black crepe carried the bodies to the church in the port for a public funeral.

The victims were buried in individual plots in various cemeteries, but a large monument in the shape of a pyramid was erected in their honor at the entrance of the Cemetery of the Chateau.

Second Opera House Shakes it Up

February 1885, four years after the disastrous fire, the new opera house – the one we see today – was opened. This time it was fitted with electric lights instead of gas and was equipped with more exits to make it safer and easier to evacuate in case of an emergency. The terrible fire was still fresh in everyone's mind.

Only three weeks after the inauguration of the new opera house, the safety features were put to the test. During a carnival ball, the building started to tremble, the huge chandelier swayed, the lights flickered and fear gripped those in attendance. But this structure was well equipped

with emergency exists and everyone was quickly evacuated without problem. The opera house withstood the
earthquake, but the public's love for the lyrical arts was
shaken. No one was in much of a hurry to go back to the
opera and performances had little attendance for the rest
of the year.

Eventually people forgot about the fire and the earthquake, and opera once again grew in popularity. The hey-
day for the *Opera de Nice*, as it's known today, was in the
twentieth century. After the Second World War, up until
the 1980s, opera was so loved that people would stand in
line all day to buy a ticket. (Remember the days before
buying tickets online?)

Even though the aristocratic winter tourists and the
eccentrics of the lost generation are long gone, the opera
house is still a place of entertainment for those who live in
Nice as well as for the thousands of tourists who visit each
year.

What to See

♦ *Opéra de Nice*, 4 Rue Saint François de Paule in the Old
Town.

♦ **Pyramid monument**, *Cimetière du Château* on Allée
François Aragon – In the cemetery on Castle Hill, there
is a large, pyramid-shaped monument to those who died
in the opera house fire. It's found in the center near the
entrance. There are also many other interesting monuments to see here, and there is a Jewish cemetery just next
to it.

♦ **Auer** – Maison Auer, 7 Rue St. François de Paule. If you are visiting the opera, don't miss the sweetshop just across the street. Maison Auer has been in the same family since 1820 and you will find some pretty tempting treats inside. But the architecture is really wonderful and it's said that the same architect that built the opera house designed the interior decoration of this shop as well.

Fun Facts

♦ **More name-dropping** – Some of the heads of state that visited the opera in Nice: King Victor-Emmanuel, King of Italy; Napoleon III; Tsar Alexander, who came in late and the performance was stopped to honor him by playing the Russian national anthem; Louis I of Bavaria; the King of Denmark; the King of Sweden; and at least four French presidents – Carnot, Faure, Loubet, and Deschanel.

♦ *Diacosmie* – The opera house also contains a *diacosmie* which is a space dedicated to everything necessary for performances. There are workshops for creating scene décor and others for costume making. Then there are storage rooms to stock the completed works. There are dedicated rehearsal rooms for the choir, the orchestra, and the ballet. There is also a room which is the exact size of the opera house stage for rehearsals with the actual props and in the same conditions. There is another room which is the same size and layout as the stage in the Acropolis, the other municipal entertainment venue.

♦ Jazz – In 1948, during the first jazz festival in Nice (which was also the first international jazz festival in the world) performances were held in the Nice opera house, as well as in the Municipal Casino and the Negresco Hotel.

♦ Observatory – The observatory which you can see in the hills behind Nice was a joint project between two great architects who are loosely associated with the *Opera de Nice*. The observatory was built by Charles Garnier and Gustav Eiffel. Garnier is responsible for the buildings and the base of the large dome and Eiffel constructed the dome itself which houses the large telescope.

War Crimes and
Liberation

Liberated, Proud and Glorious

In the summertime, Nice is humming with activity. Tourists are everywhere, cafés are full, music fills the air, and everyone seems to be having a good time. In this festive atmosphere it's difficult to imagine that not so very long ago (1940-1945), this city, as well as the rest of France, was under German occupation and the mood was very different.

On Avenue Jean Médecin, just at the north end of Galleries Lafayette, you will find two plaques that remind us it wasn't always so pleasant here. The arcades on each side of the street are named after two Resistance fighters who were hanged during World War II.

It was June 1944 and the American troops had landed in Provence. The Resistance activities in Nice escalated and two German soldiers and a colonel were killed. The occupiers decided to teach the people a lesson, so they went to the village of Gattières, near Grasse, and rounded up all of the men. They selected two who were suspected of being members of the Resistance and brought them to Nice to make an example. They were imprisoned and tortured before being condemned to death by a military tribunal situated in Hotel Ruhl (where Casino Ruhl is today).

The two men were Ange Grassi, a 40-year-old Italian mason and Séraphin Torrin, a 32-year-old farmer from Provence. On July 7, the two men were hanged from the streetlights just in front of where the two plaques are located. Then the population was forced to file past the hanging bodies. It's said that some of the Niçois came back in the night and placed flowers at the sites. These two men become symbols of the Resistance and today the arcades bear their names, Arcade Grassi and Arcade Torrin.

However, their executions didn't have the effect the Germans had hoped for. Instead of weakening the Resistance, it grew stronger. In late August, the American army was just across the Var River from Nice. A Resistance messenger sneaked across the river at night and came back with some bad news. The American general had decided that instead of crossing the Var and coming into Nice, he would go in another direction. The Niçois decided they couldn't wait any longer and took things into their own hands.

On August 28 there was a violent general uprising against the Germans and the 2,000 or so troops (those that were not taken prisoner or killed in the battle) fled the city. Two days later, when the Americans learned that Nice had liberated itself, they came in to make sure the city stayed secured and to pursue the fleeing German troops. When they arrived, there wasn't a bottle of champagne to be found in the city because the liberation celebration had already taken place. The Niçois happily welcomed the American forces anyway.

Every year on August 28, Nice celebrates its liberation. The city is overrun by old army vehicles from World War II, soldiers in uniform, American flags and, of course, the remaining few who were here in 1944 and their descendants. Patriotism and thankfulness fill the air and the words of General de Gaulle come to mind, **"Liberated Nice, Proud Nice, Glorious Nice."**

What to See

♦ **Plaques** – The plaques honoring Grassi and Torrin are located at the intersection of Avenue Jean Médecin and Rue des Hôtel des Postes and Rue de la Liberté.

Translated, they read: *Ange Grassi/Séraphin Torrin "French Resistance fighters, members of FFI (Interior French Forces) were hanged here July 7, 1944 and left exposed for having resisted the Hitlerien oppression. Passerby, bow your head and remember."*

And Nice does remember. Every year on July 7, at sunset, the Committee of Memory of the Resistance (Comité du Souvenir de la Résistance) commemorates their deaths by laying flowers at the place where they were hanged.

♦ **Resistance Plaques** – There are many smaller plaques all around the city honoring those who fought and died in the resistance. Notice these plaques as you stroll around.

♦ **World War II Jewish deportation** – In front of the Excelsior Hotel, 19 Avenue Durante, there is a plaque which reads:

"During the German occupation of Nice from September 1943 through August 1944, more than 3,000 Jews including 264 children were arrested in the Alpes-Maritimes, the Lower Alpes, and the Principality of Monaco and deported by the Gestapo in accordance with the Nazi anti-Semitic ideology.

Before being transferred by train to the camp in Drancy near Paris from where they were led to the extermination camp of Auschwitz, the victims were interred in the Hotel Excelsior which had become an annex of the Drancy camp and requisitioned by the Germans because of its proximity to the railway station of Nice.

Inaugurated October 9, 2009 by Christian Estrosi, Minister of Industry, Mayor of Nice, President of Nice Côte d'Azur in the presence of Serge Klarsfeild and Eric Ciotti, Deputy President of the General Counsil of the Alpes-Maritimes."

♦ **First World War Monument** – The monument at the foot of the *Colline du Château* (Castle Hill) facing the sea was built 1924-1928 on the site of an old quarry, and honors the people of Nice who died in the First World War. In the center is an urn containing 3,665 plaques, each bearing the name of a life lost in the war. On either side is a high-relief sculpture by Alfred Janniot, the sculptor responsible for the Apollo Sun Fountain in Place Massena. The sculpture on the left represents war and the one on the right, peace.

Casino Wars

An Unsolved Murder Mystery

In the 1970s, Nice was in the middle of what the press dubbed the Casino Wars. The mayor was the ambitious and corrupt Jacques Médecin (son of Jean Médecin). Jacques had modern ideas and planned to make Nice the "Las Vegas of the Riviera" – with a little help from his buddy, Jean-Dominique Fratoni, a shady Corsican with ties to the Mafia.

At that time, the city had a beautiful municipal casino, on Place Massena just in front of where the jets of water are now. The lease on the building had run out, it had reverted to the city, and the mayor decided to tear it down.

At the same time, another beautiful building on the Promenade was being torn down and the mayor chose that site for a new hotel and casino. A thoroughly modern building (the one we see today) was constructed in the Las Vegas style of the 1970s and Casino Ruhl was opened in 1974 by Fratoni. Fratoni bought into the mayor's idea and decided that he would become the "Godfather of Gambling" in the new "Las Vegas of the Riviera."

As every good gangster knows, the first thing you must do to monopolize the market is to eliminate the competition. He set his eye on his nearest competitor, the Palais de la Méditerranée, a hotel and casino housed in a stunning art deco building just a bit further along the promenade.

Soon after Fratoni's casino opened, the other casinos started to have a "run of bad luck." In 1975, a group of five men entered the Palais de la Méditerranée and won five million francs (more than $1 million at the time). Then, a bit later, the very same thing happened at Sun Beach Casino in Menton – and at least one of the men was present at both "winnings". The Menton casino lost three million francs, which put them in a precarious financial state. So Fratoni came to the rescue. He kindly bailed them out... and then he kindly took over their casino.

The Palais de la Méditerranée was also in terrible distress after its huge loss. The CEO resigned and all the directors thought they had no choice but to close or give in to Fratoni who was offering to bail them out in return for control of the casino.

What can I say? I'm just a nice guy who tries to help out his fellow casino owners when they hit hard times.

But then a formidable woman stepped up. Her name was Renée Le Roux and her family had a 50% share in the casino. She was a widow in her early fifties with four adult children when she became CEO.

The Palais de la Méditerranée had 380 employees who would lose their jobs if the casino closed, and Madame Le Roux was determined not to let that happen. She was convinced that with hard work the casino could recover, and she wasn't one to give in to bullying – not even from the Mafia. She took a bank loan to cover their huge loss and then got to work getting the casino back on its feet. All the employees pulled together with her to make it work.

And it might have worked if Madame Le Roux's daughter hadn't shown up. Agnes was returning from Africa where her marriage had dissolved. She was 29, troubled, and was demanding her inheritance from her mother. Madame Le Roux refused and conflict ensued.

Fratoni was quick to recognize Agnes as his opponent's weak spot. He sent in Maurice Agnelet who was quite the lady's man and always had several mistresses. He showed an interest in Agnes and soon had her swooning for him. Then, on behalf of Fratoni, he convinced her to vote against her mother at a board meeting, which would allow Fratoni to take control of the casino. Fratoni paid Agnes three million francs for her vote and for her shares which she was to transfer to him.

With Madame Le Roux out of the picture, Fratoni took control of the Palais de la Méditerranée and, claiming it was losing money, started making preparations to close it down. Madame Le Roux was stunned by her daughter's betrayal and the loss of her business. But things were about to get even worse.

The money Fratoni paid Agnes went into her joint account with Maurice Agnelet in Switzerland. A few months later Maurice moved the money into his own personal account.

Soon after Agnes voted against her mother and received the payoff, Maurice broke off their relationship. Agnes was devastated and supposedly tried to commit suicide twice, although police described the circumstances as suspicious. Then a few months later, in October 1977, after a reconciliation with Maurice, Agnes planned to spend the weekend with him in Italy. That weekend she disappeared without a trace and has never been seen or heard from again.

Madame Le Roux immediately accused Maurice Agnelet of kidnapping and murder and claimed the whole thing was planned by Fratoni to eliminate competition for his casino, Casino Ruhl.

At Madame Le Roux's insistence, Maurice Agnelet was brought to trial in 1985. But since Agnes's body had never been found and he had an alibi for the weekend that she went missing, the case was dismissed. But Madame Le Roux wasn't about to give up. All the energy that she had put into keeping the casino afloat was transferred into the search for the truth about what happened to her daughter and she continued to investigate and bring accusations against Maurice Agnelet.

He was brought to trial again in 2006 and acquitted. But when it was later discovered that his former mistress had lied about him being with her that fateful weekend, he was re-tried in 2007, found guilty, and sentenced to 20 years in prison.

Maurice Agnelet's attorney took the case to the European Court of Human Rights and, in 2013, it was decided that he had not had a fair trial. So in 2014, a 76-year-old Maurice Agnelet was back in the courtroom.

I tell you, she gave me that money. Just before she... disappeared.

This time, his son volunteered to testify against him. He said that his father had confessed privately to him and that his mother had also told him that his father had killed Agnes. Both parents denied his claims and said their son was unstable. However, the court upheld the previous 20-year sentence and Maurice went back to prison vowing to continue his appeals.

At 92 years old, Madame Le Roux was not able to attend this trial. Her son and two daughters appeared in her place. The Le Roux family considers this affair finally over. Even if Maurice Agnelet should be freed or have another trial, for them, Madame Le Roux's 36 years of labor is finished. Their only regret is that they still don't know the whereabouts of Agnes's body.

Madame Le Roux wrote a book with her son in 1989 called Une femme face à la Mafia, or "One Woman Against the Mafia". In 2014 the book was made into a film called L'homme qu'on aimait trop, or "The Man They Loved Too

Much" with Catherine Deneuve playing the formidable Madame Le Roux.

What about the money?

As of 2015, the three million francs that has now become 3.2 million euros is still tied up in Switzerland, as it has been since 1978. Three parties have claims on it.

♦ **Maurice Agnelet** – Maurice Agnelet claims the money was a gift to him from Agnes, the very person he is in prison for murdering.

♦ **Fratoni** – Jean-Dominique Fratoni, nicknamed the "Godfather of Gambling" was suspected of being involved in the disappearance of Agnes. He fled to Switzerland, but was sentenced in absentia to five years prison and fined 410 million francs for financial irregularities. He placed a claim on the money in 1981 maintaining that he had paid the money to Agnes for her vote against her mother and for the transfer of her shares in the casino. She disappeared before the shares were transferred, so he felt he was due a refund. He died in 1994 but his will designated that the funds go to the Red Cross and the Cancer Research Foundation and they are still pursing the funds.

♦ **Family** – Then, of course, there is the family of Agnes Le Roux that wants to keep the money out of the hands of those responsible for her death. They say it should go to her family who has spent a fortune trying to discover her fate and bring the guilty parties to justice. In 2013 a judgment was passed in favor of the family but the other two parties appealed it.

And the casinos?

♦ Palais de la Méditerranée – When Fratoni took control from Madame Le Roux, he set about closing down the casino. However, the 380 employees who had stood with Madame Le Roux had acquired a bit of her stubbornness. They staged a sit-in from April 1978 until January 1981. For almost three years (998 days) they occupied the building and refused to let authorities enter. They draped the building in banners and put an old player piano out front to attract attention. They passed out flyers and tried to get public support to save the casino. Finally the police entered when the picketers were asleep and the former employees had to give up their dream of saving the casino.

The building sat empty and deteriorating for years and was set to be razed in the 1980s. Thankfully, a handful of writers and artists campaigned to save the beautiful art deco structure which had been built in 1929 by American businessman, Frank J. Gould. In 1989 the façade was classed as a historic monument and narrowly escaped the wrecking ball. However, the rest of the building was demolished and rebuilt. It reopened in 2004.

♦ Casino Ruhl – The casino was closed by the State from 1982-1987 for financial irregularities and unpaid taxes. It reopened in 1987 under new management.

And the mayor?

Jacques Médecin was mayor of Nice from 1965-1990. He was convicted of several counts of corruption (not necessarily related to this incident) and in order to escape going to prison he fled to Uruguay in 1990. He was extradited in 1994, then in a court mix-up he was given a suspended sentence instead of being sent to prison. He hotfooted it back to Uruguay where he stayed until his death in 1998. Aside from his corruption charges, he's remembered as the author of a popular Niçois cookbook.

What to See

♦ Casino Ruhl, 1 Promenade des Anglais

♦ Palais de la Méditerranée, 13 Promenade des Anglais

♦ Promenade du Paillon – As you stroll through the Promenade du Paillon, you will notice signs indicating the names of various sections of the park. One such section is called *Espace Jacques Médecin*. Naming an area of the park after a mayor who left the city with a lot of debt and who was convicted of financial wrongdoing was controversial, but supporters of the idea say that Mr. Médecin also did many good things for the city.

Fun Facts

Besides the two casinos you've read about here, Nice had two other casinos.

♦ The Municipal Casino was located in Place Massena from 1884-1964. During the Second World War, it was turned into a storage area for people who had been evacuated from war-torn areas. The Italian troops were the first to arrive in Nice and when they rolled into the city and saw the magnificent casino building in the main plaza, they were sure it was City Hall. They captured the uniformed guard of the casino-turned-storage facility and demanded to see the Mayor. This at least gave the Niçois something to laugh about during the war.

♦ The Casino Jetée Promenade sat on a pier in the sea across from Casino Ruhl from 1891 to 1944. It was a magnificent glass and iron structure with a glass dome 20 meters (65 feet) high inspired by the Crystal Palace which was built in London for the 1851 World's Fair. During the Second World War, the Italians stripped it of all copper, bronze, brass wiring and electric cables. Then the Germans came in and finished it off. They used the iron and glass to form barricades along the beach because they thought the Allies would come through Africa into the south of France.

Bank Robbery
of the Century

In July 1976, La Société Générale, a bank in Nice, was robbed. The event was later dubbed the "Bank Robbery of the Century", or La Casse du Siècle. It gained a lot of media attention, not only because of the amount stolen (they made off with fifty million francs, or about thirty million euros), but also because of the way it was carried out.

The Sewer Gang

A group of about fifteen men dug a tunnel 8 meters (26 feet) long from the sewers of Nice to the bank vault. Their underground escapades earned them the nickname the Sewer Gang.

They took to the drains disguised as city workers in florescent yellow overalls. After three months of slipping around in the sewers, they were under the bank. To help them find the location of the vault containing the bank's safe deposit boxes, they rented one and placed an alarm clock inside. They set the alarm to go off in the middle of the night to help them pinpoint the exact location of the vault. It also served as a test to make sure the bank didn't have a security system that picked up on sound or vibration. This was an important consideration since they intended to smash through a 1.8 meter (6 feet) thick concrete wall and would probably be making some noise and causing a bit of vibration.

Over the weekend of July 16–18, 1976, they broke through the floor. The first thing they did was solder shut the metal vault door from the inside so no one could surprise them. Then the Sewer Gang spent the weekend breaking into 371 safe deposit boxes while picnicking on foie gras and red wine. On Sunday it started to rain and they had wrap up their weekend picnic activities and get all of their loot out before the rising water in the sewers trapped them.

But before leaving, they wrote a note on the wall. Each letter was written by a different person so the handwriting couldn't be traced. It said, "Ni armes, ni violence et sans haine" or "Neither weapons nor violence, and without hate." They thought leaving this message showing their goodwill might work in their favor – just in case they were caught.

Monday morning when the bank opened, the employees found the vault door sealed shut from the inside. When they finally got it open they couldn't believe what they saw. The police investigated, but the Sewer Gang left no clues. Several suspects were arrested but had to be released for lack of evidence. For the most part, the criminals laid low and kept quiet. But there was one among them who liked the limelight and just couldn't keep his daring deeds to himself. His name was Albert Spaggiari, called Bert.

Albert (Bert) Spaggiari

Bert had grown up in the South of France. At seventeen, he joined the parachutists in Indochina where he began his criminal career. He was convicted there and sent back to France to serve time in prison.

After his release, he went to work in a factory in Senegal that produced safe deposit boxes. As part of his job, Bert often had to break into those strongboxes for clients who had lost their keys. This provided great training for his future career path. After mastering the art of breaking into safes, he returned to France and was again arrested and sent to prison.

After his second prison term, he moved to the hills behind Nice and started a law-abiding career, working as photographer for the city of Nice. But in his spare time, Bert liked to read crime novels. There was one in particular that fascinated him. It was called Tous à l'égout by Robert Pollock (in English it was titled "Loophole, or How to Rob a Bank"). It was an inspiring novel about a gang who used the sewers to tunnel under a bank and rob it. An idea was born!

Bert just happened to have a friend who worked at the Société Générale Bank in Nice, and after a few inquiries, he learned that there was no alarm in the bank's safe. The thick concrete walls were considered impenetrable. But after reading his inspirational book and finding a vault with no alarm, Bert just couldn't resist – and the rest, as they say, is history.

Immediately after the robbery, Bert went to the US. He offered his services to the CIA, claiming as his credentials that he was the brains behind the "Bank Robbery of the Century." Surprisingly, the CIA declined his generous offer and he returned to France. He must have thought the CIA had an oath of confidentiality (like lawyers and doctors) because he didn't even consider that they might notify the French authorities – but they did.

About the same time, a couple of small-time criminals, who had acted as lookouts and were paid in gold from the robbery, were caught trying to cash in their marked gold bars. They quickly confessed and named Bert as the mastermind of the heist.

In the meantime, Bert, as official photographer for the city, had gone on a trip to Japan with Jacques Médecin, then mayor of Nice. (Remember him from the Casino Wars?) When Bert returned, the police were waiting at the airport to arrest him. After two days in jail, he confessed, claiming that he was the head of the operation but would give no other names. This seemed to solve everything. The police had their bank robber, Bert had his fame, and the others had their money. Everyone was happy.

But Bert wasn't finished. Five months later, he was appearing in front of a judge when he escaped by jumping out a window of the courthouse, the Palais du Justice in the Old Town of Nice. He bounced off the top of a car, then jumped onto the back of a waiting motorcycle and disappeared.

As Bert was making his escape, the judge condemned him to life imprisonment. But Bert never went back to prison because he was never caught. For the rest of his life, he was on the run. He traveled a lot, mostly in South America but he did go back to France occasionally. Afraid of being recognized, he had plastic surgery in Argentina and often wore disguises. Although he didn't want to be caught, he didn't want to be forgotten either. He regularly sent photos of himself to the newspapers – sometimes dressed as Santa Claus or wearing some other disguise.

In 1978, Bert wrote about the crime in his book Les Egouts du paradis or "The Sewers of Paradise." In it, he claimed the heist was completely his idea. He explored the sewers and then contacted two men from Marseille to put together a team. However, the police who had investigated the crime always considered his book a work of fiction. His claims just didn't line up with the evidence.

Bert died in Italy in 1989, with the world knowing only his version of the story. But the statue of limitations on this crime has run out and now the others who participated are old and want to brag a bit too. At least two of them have written books detailing the bank robbery events. Both of them claim that Bert was not the head of the operation, although one of them admits that he probably thought he was.

What to See

♦ *Palais du Justice* (Court House) in the Old Town ‑This is where Bert jumped out the window, got onto the back of a waiting motorcycle and disappeared into the underground parking lot. Once underground he was moved into the trunk of a car and was driven out.

♦ Société Générale, 8 Avenue Jean Médecin – the bank that the Sewer Gang robbed is still open in Nice, but I'm pretty sure they now have an alarm system.

Fun Facts

♦ **Accuse the Mayor** – At the time of writing, Christian Estrosi is the mayor of Nice, but in 1977, when Bert escaped, the young Mr. Estrosi was a professional motorcycle racer. In 1995, eighteen years after Bert's escape, Jacques Peyrat, who had been Bert's attorney and was now Estrosi's political rival, accused Estrosi of being the motorcyclist who drove off with Bert. But Mr. Estrosi's alibi was easy enough to prove – on that day he was participating in a race in Daytona.

♦ **Books** – Two members of the Sewer Gang have now written books about the bank robbery:
– *La Vérité sur la Casse de Nice* in French by Jacques Cassandri. Even though he used the pen name of "Amigo" he was easily recognized.
– *Confessions d'un Braqueur* in French by Didier Caulier.
– *Cinq Milliards au bout de l'égout* is a 1977 French book by René Louis Maurice and Jean-Claude Simoën. It has been translated into English under the titles, *The Heist of the Century*, *The Gentleman of 16 July*, and *Under the Streets of Nice*.

♦ **Movies**
– *The Great Riviera Bank Robbery*, British (1979)
– *Les égouts du paradis*, French (1979)
– *Sans arme, ni haine, ni violence*, French (2008)

Apollo Fountain

∞

A Greek God just can't get any Respect

When a powerful Greek deity arrives in Nice, he is ridiculed, humiliated, and banned from the city.

If you visit Place Massena, in the very heart of Nice, you will see a large fountain called the *Fontaine du Soleil,* or "Sun Fountain." There are five bronze sculptures in the basin and in the center stands an impressive marble Apollo. He is seven meters (23 ft.) tall and weighs in at seven tons. He is definitely the king of the square and you would think this giant would be admired and respected... but not by the Niçois.

When the Sun Fountain was unveiled in 1956, the people of Nice were not at all impressed. Apollo's job, according to mythology, is to carry the sun across the sky every day, and he usually does this in his chariot pulled by four horses. But this Apollo didn't have a chariot and the four horses were on top of his head, forming a sort of crown.

The citizens of Nice claimed he looked like an advertisement for the most popular automobile at the time, the Renault 4CV, known as the *quatre chevaux*, or "four horsepower." So the magnificent Greek deity was saddled with the nickname, "the four horsepower statue."

But there was a bigger problem, and it was located further down the nude sculpture. Some conservative inhabitants of the city thought his "manhood" was too large, while some older ladies thought it was too small, and college students took to decorating it as a prank.

In an effort to calm the controversy, the sculptor took a hammer and chisel to his creation to reduce the size of the offending member. This operation earned Apollo a new nickname. Now, instead of being called "four horsepower," he was called "the virgin."

Even the embarrassing surgery to which Apollo was subjected proved to be insufficient. It wasn't enough to satisfy the Catholic women's "League of Feminine Virtue." He was still nude as were the bronze statues. The virtuous women gained so much support that in the 1970s, the fountain with its naked sculptures was dismantled.

The bronze figures were stored at the water treatment plant and Apollo went to stand guard over the mayor's office for a short time before being moved out of the city center to stand near a sport stadium where he was less likely to offend the ladies. He stayed there for about thirty years.

In 2007, a reporter researching water treatment spotted the bronze statues at the purification station. He wrote an article about the fate of the Sun Fountain and the public took an interest in it. The fountain was reinstalled with the bronze sculptures in the basin, but the giant Apollo was still not allowed to return.

Finally in 2011, Apollo was reinstated to his rightful position. Today he stands at the center of the fountain in Place Massena proudly surveying the plaza and all of the passersby. The Sun Fountain is once again complete and as the artist intended... well, almost. Even though there is a little less of Apollo than there used to be, he's still quite an impressive sight.

Bronze Sculptures

The five bronze sculptures in the fountain represent five planets/gods:

♦ **Earth** is a woman holding a baby. An owl sits on her shoulder and she's accompanied by a bull.
♦ **Mercury** sits on his winged horse and has wings on his helmet.
♦ **Mars** is holding his horse by the nose.
♦ **Saturn** stands by a bull.
♦ **Venus** is a woman on a dolphin.

Fun Facts

♦ **Sculptor** – This fountain is the work of Alfred Janniot who is also responsible for two high-relief sculptures on the War Monument at the base of the *Colline du Château*, facing the sea.

♦ **In hiding** – Janniot had finished the bronzes, but had not yet started on Apollo when the Second World War broke out. The bronzes were buried in a garden to keep them from being destroyed, and then dug up after the war was over.

PART 4:
TASTE OF
TRADITION

Nice might seem like a typical French city, but beneath that French veneer lies a strong and proud Niçois culture. Long before Nice was French, it was Niçois and it has held on to its own language, songs, dances, traditional costumes, and food. The people of Nice work very hard at keeping their traditions alive; children learn the language and dances in school, and cultural associations keep them involved by performing at events throughout the year. We'll read about some of these traditional Niçois festivals later in this section.

Language

The local language is called *Niçois* in French or *Nissart* in Niçois. It's a dialect of Occitan, a language which was spoken in the south of France in the Middle Ages. When Nice separated from Provence in 1388, it gradually developed its own dialect which over time became the Niçois language spoken today and seen on street signs in the Old Town.

The people of Nice were speaking Niçois even way back when they were being shuffled between Savoy and France. Maybe this is why they weren't too bothered about whose jurisdiction they were under. They just went about their daily business speaking Niçois. They've been writing songs, poems, and stories in Niçois continuously since the Middle Ages so the language has never died out.

Costumes

If you attend a Niçois event, one of the things that will probably impress you the most is the colorful, distinctive costumes of the dancers. These traditional garments were quickly disappearing around the first part of the twentieth century when the young were eager to wear modern styles and latest fashions.

In 1960 the County of Nice was preparing to celebrate the centennial of its reattachment to France (the second vote of 1860). The deputy-mayor of Nice, Jean Médecin, asked the mayors of all communities in the Alpes-Maritimes Department to send any information they could collect about their traditional costumes. The results were meager and disappointing, so Mr. Médecin contacted Gustave-Adolphe Mossa, curator of the fine arts museum, and asked him to document the Niçois costume. Luckily, the museum held some rich resources. The nineteenth-century painters had found the local costumes very romantic and they preserved them for us in their paintings. Mossa's project was fruitful and the results were used to create the costumes worn by the traditional dance groups.

The flower-seller and fisherman costumes are two that are often used in dance performances.

Dance Groups

There are two main folkloric dance groups in Nice: *Ciamada Nissarda* and *Nice la Belle*. The first one, *Ciamada Nissarda*, started in 1925 as a theatre group, performing plays in Niçois. Later, they started giving traditional dance performances. The second group, *Nice la Belle* was formed in 1955 by Francis Gag at the request of the mayor, Jean Médecin. In the 1960s and 1970s, these groups started giving classes for young people and at the end of the 1970s, traditional dance classes began to be offered in the schools.

Flower Seller   **Fisherman**

Gourd Festival

C∞

101 Things to Do with a Gourd

The first Niçois festival to take place during the year is the *Festin des Cougourdon* (Gourd Festival). *Cougourdon* is the Niçois name for the special type of gourd that is so dear to the hearts of the people of Nice. This inedible fruit was introduced to the region in the sixteenth century and is so important that it has its own festival. This is the perfect place to see all things Niçois. You can sample the traditional food, enjoy the music and dance, and, of course, discover numerous ways to decorate a gourd.

This celebration is actually associated with the religious festival of the Annunciation, although it's not really clear what gourds have to do with God announcing to Mary that she's going to have a baby. But I guess it's as good a time as any to celebrate the gourd. The festival is held in the Park of Cimiez, near the Church of the Monastery where Mary is the patron saint. Since the date of the

Annunciation is March 25, the gourd festival is on the Sunday closest to that date.

Historically, the gourd contributed in many ways to Niçois life. The vines were used on trellises to shade patios and windows from the hot Mediterranean sun. Then, when the long bulbous fruit was dried it could be used as a flask to carry water or wine out into the fields (and reportedly keep them at a constant temperature), or made into a variety of lightweight, waterproof kitchen utensils.

Today, most of our lightweight, waterproof kitchen utensils are made of plastic instead of gourd, but the festival that started in the Middle Ages to celebrate this useful fruit continues. In the late 1800s, when the newfound tourism industry was booming, the Niçois started decorating the gourds and selling them to tourists. These painted gourds made great souvenirs of a visit to Nice. It's said that even Queen Victoria, who used to stay just across the street and ride her little donkey cart through the park, bought a few of them herself. (I wonder if they might still be in the Royal Archives somewhere.) Today, we continue to enjoy gourds as works of art and their unusual shapes inspire artists to come up with countless ways to decorate them. So, if you've been wondering what you could do with a gourd, the gourd festival is the place to go for inspiration.

Festival of Reproach

Historically the Gourd Festival had another interesting aspect. It was also known as the Festival of Reproach. It was a time when couples could publicly air their grievances with one another after having been cooped up together in close quarters all winter. The community would then encourage them to kiss and make up and all would be well.

According to Niçois folklore, the gourd brings good luck and there's a saying that "A home without a gourd is like an empty nest." An old tradition says that you should buy a gourd in the autumn and let it dry in the house over the winter. However, you must be very careful not to say things you shouldn't in its presence because in the past, gourds have been known to tell all at the Festival of Reproach.

What to See

In the park of Cimiez, 160 Avenue des Arènes:

♦ **Monastery, Church, Cemetery, and Gardens** – This Franciscan monastery is still home to a small group of monks as it has been since the sixteenth century. If you're interested in the Franciscan monastic lifestyle, you can learn all about it in a small museum in the complex. In the church you can see three important works by the medieval Niçois artist, Louis Brea and the cemetery is the final resting place of artists Henri Matisse and Raoul Dufy.

♦ **Jazz** – For several years the Jazz Festival of Nice was held in this garden. The pathways through the park bear jazz-inspired names and you will find statues of Louis Armstrong and other jazz artists near the entrance.

♦ **Museums** – The Matisse Museum, 164 Avenue des Arènes, is in the park in a large salmon-colored seventeenth-century house and the Chagall Museum is nearby on Avenue du Docteur Ménard.

♦ **Roman Ruins** – Visit the ruins of the former Roman city of Cemenelum in the park.

Fun Facts

♦ Dragon of Cimiez – From the seventeenth century up until 1857 there was a dragon in the church of the monastery of Cimiez. The story goes that there was a terrible dragon in the area that was eating children and terrorizing adults. The monks of the monastery prayed for help and an angel appeared and slew the dragon. The heavenly visitor then suspended the dead beast from the ceiling of the church for all to see.

Well, as you might have guessed, that wasn't the real story. It seems that a group of European explorers including a few Niçois were traveling in Egypt in the seventeenth century. They were on the banks of the Nile River when they were surprised by some crocodiles. The Niçois men prayed (fervently we imagine) to the Virgin of Cimiez. The men succeeded in killing the beasts and brought one of them back to the church in Cimiez as a sign of thanks. During the two centuries that it hung in the church, the crocodile story was forgotten and the dragon story was invented. The dragon/crocodile was finally removed in 1857 when someone realized that it might be scaring people away.

Vespa Band

Something Else to Do with a Gourd

In the last chapter, we discovered that a cougourdon is a type of gourd grown in the south of France that can be fashioned into many useful and decorative objects. But another, unexpected use for these dried fruits is making music with them. We don't see them much today, but in the past there were entire bands made of nothing but gourd-based instruments.

Since gourds come in all different shapes and sizes, so do the instruments made from them. You'll find some shaped like drums, tubas, flutes, and others that would be difficult to put a name to. However, the most typical instrument in the *vespa* band is the *petadou*. It's a friction drum made from half a gourd with the opening covered by tightly stretched leather. A hole in the middle of the leather allows a reed to be rhythmically raised and lowered to make music. The name, *petadou*, comes from the French word *"pet"* which means "a fart." So you can probably imagine the sound this instrument makes.

But what about the rest of the instruments, what do they sound like? You might imagine that the music produced by a bunch of gourds wouldn't be very melodic... and you'd be right. These bands are called *vespa* for a reason. *Vespa* is the Niçois (and Italian) word for wasp. They were tagged with this name because they sound quite similar to a swarm of buzzing wasps (and the little Italian scooter with the same name).

Traditionally, these *vespa* bands performed during the carnival for a bit of buffoonery. But maybe there was another purpose. People once believed that at carnival time, the spirits of the dead mixed among the living. To protect themselves and keep one of these spirits from entering them, people donned costumes and masks to cover their face and body. But the exposed ears were protected by the buzzing sound of the *vespa* band.

These bands were very popular at the end of the 1800s and early 1900s but started to disappear in the 1960s. Today, as there is more and more interest in the Niçois culture and language perhaps we will soon see these buzzing bands return to the carnival celebration.

What to See

♦ **Palais Lascaris,** 15 Rue Droite – While it's unlikely that you'll see a vespa band in Nice, if you are interested in musical instruments, Palais Lascaris in the Old Town has a collection of more typical antique instruments (of the non-gourd type) that you might find interesting.

Listening to my music can keep spirits out of your ears!

May Festivals

$\sim\!\!\infty\!\!\sim$

The Merry Month of May

The second Niçois festival of the year is called *la fête des mai* and it's celebrated every weekend in the month of May. This is in addition to all the regular May holidays – and there are certainly plenty of those. Some years, May has as many as four public holidays plus Mother's Day. You would think that would be enough for anyone, but not for the Niçois.

Their traditional celebration is called *la fête des mai* in French or *lu mai* in the Niçois language. Every weekend is a celebration of all things Niçois. There is traditional music and dance, colorful, historic costumes, lots of characteristic Niçois food, and fun activities designed to help young and old learn the language and understand the culture of Nice.

For centuries these festivities were held in the middle of each neighborhood. The central square or crossroad would be decorated and it became the hub of activity. But in the early twentieth century, the increase in automobiles and traffic meant that this tradition was at risk of being lost. So to allow the Niçois to continue their celebrations and to not block the traffic every weekend in May, it was decided to have one large festival, in the park in Cimiez.

It makes for a great family day out. You can pack a picnic lunch or buy food there and eat among the ancient olive trees. There are activities to keep the children occupied, like bouncy castles, puppet shows, and games. Nearby you'll find the monastery and its gardens, Roman ruins, and the Matisse Museum.

What is a Mai?

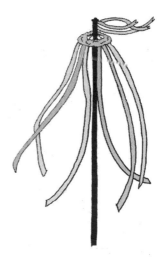

In a tradition that goes back to the time of the Romans, the arrival of Spring was celebrated by cutting down a tree which would then be placed in a temple and decorated with flowers. This "May tree" became known as a *mai*. The tradition evolved into putting the mai in the center of each neighborhood and dancing around it. Today, instead of cutting down trees every year, we use a tall pole (a maypole) decorated with ribbons.

More Niçois Celebrations

The Gourd Festival and the May Festivals are the two largest Niçois celebrations, but there are several others sprinkled throughout the year. They are largely religious in origin and celebrated in churches, but the traditional music, dance, and costumes are usually included. The dates for most of these celebrations fluctuate because they are typically held on a Sunday.

Fête du Vœu (Celebration of the Vow) — May

In the early 1830s a deadly cholera epidemic was sweeping through France and parts of Europe. Nice was Sardinian at the time and located just across the Var River from cholera-infested France. Everyone was worried. The Niçois officials got together and made a vow (*un vœu*) to the Virgin, that if she would protect the city from the epidemic, they would build a new church dedicated to her. The *vœu* was officially adopted by the city council on April 25, 1832.

The city was, indeed, spared from cholera and the church was built. It was started in 1835 and finished in 1852. L'Eglise Notre Dame des Grâces sits on Place Saint Jean Baptiste. It's easily spotted from the east end of the Promenade du Paillon near the National Theatre. Every year, usually in the month of May, there is a remembrance ceremony. It starts with a procession through the Old Town, then goes to Place Saint François (where the fish market is held). There, in front of the old city hall where the first vow was written, the mayor reads the original *vœu* in Niçois. The procession then goes to the church where a mass is held. During the mass, the mayor renews the vow of placing Nice under the protection of the Madonna of the Graces. This celebration is also accompanied by traditional Niçois music and dance.

Fête de la Saint Pierre — June

This annual celebration has been held since the Middle Ages when being a fisherman was a very dangerous occupation. Fishermen counted on Saint Peter, their patron saint, to protect them from storms and pirates. Every year they met to honor their protector. They would gather in the evening on the beach around the boat of the poorest fisherman among them... and burn it. It wasn't as cruel as it sounds though, because then they would present him with a brand new boat and ask Saint Peter to protect them and give them a spirit of brotherhood in the coming year.

In the month of June, the Saint Peter's celebration still takes place at the port in Nice. It starts with a mass in the church of Notre Dame du Port in Place de l'Île de Beauté. Then a statue of Saint Peter is carried in a procession to the port. There the officials get into boats for a little procession on the sea where they throw out wreaths. Then a boat is burned to honor the old custom. The mayor is usually in attendance and there are traditional Niçois costumes and music.

ST. PETER'S DAY
The only time it's best to be the poorest

Fête du Malonat — July

In 1854, about twenty years after Nice was saved from the cholera epidemic by the Madonna of Graces (see La Fête du Vœu above), the deadly disease came back to threaten the Niçois. The area in the Old Town around Rue Malonat (an extension of Rue de la Préfecture) followed the example of the city, went to the Virgin for help, and the epidemic began to recede. But since they were just a small quarter of the Old Town – just a few streets, really – they couldn't afford to build a church. The best they could offer the Madonna was a shrine at the end of the street.

They collected money and built a shrine to house a statue honoring their savior. The shrine of Notre Dame du Malonat stands at the end of Rue Malonat. Every year since 1854 a celebration of thanksgiving has taken place. On a Saturday evening, the Virgin leaves her shrine and is carried in a lighted procession through decorated streets to l'Eglise du Gésu (the church of Jesus), Rue Droite in the Old Town. The next day, after a mass in the church, there is another procession in which the statue is carried back to the end of Rue Malonat and put back in her shrine. The structure was refurbished in 1966 under the orders of the mayor, Jean Médecin.

Fête de la Saint Barthélemy — September

This is an annual fair where you can discover specialties from the County of Nice and surrounding regions. You can buy local products and taste traditional food while enjoying folkloric music and dance. While the location could change, it has usually been held at Place Pierre Gautier just off Cours Saleya beside the Miséricorde Chapel.

Fête de la Sainte Réparate — October

Sainte Réparate is the patron saint of Nice. Every year, a statue of Sainte Réparate is placed in a boat and carried in a procession through the Old Town. It starts at Rue de l'Hôtel de Ville and goes to the Cathedral Sainte Réparate in Place Rossetti accompanied by traditional music. A mass is said in the cathedral then wreaths are laid at the

Monument aux Morts in Place Rossetti. Later a concert is given in the Cathedral.

To read about Sainte Réparate and find out why she is in a boat, see "Bay of Angels" in Part 1.

Ceremony in Honor of
Catherine Ségurane — November

Catherine Ségurane is the heroine of Nice that we read about in Part 1 (the Niçoise laundress who saved the day). She embodies Niçois pride and patriotism. Every year on a weekend near November 25, which is Saint Catherine's Day, there's a celebration with traditional music and dance in front of the monument on Rue Sincaire. Then a religious service is held in the nearby church of Saint Martin-Saint Augustin, Place Saint Augustin. Afterward, it's back outside for more music, dancing, and drinks.

Carnival — February

Carnival is celebrated all over the world, but it's an integral part of Nice's history, as it has been celebrated in the city for hundreds of years. The earliest mention of it is from 1294. It was originally an unorganized street party, then in 1830 the King and Queen of Sardinia were in Nice and the city wanted to show off a bit, so they organized a parade. The parade took place in Cours Saleya for many years before moving to the newer areas of Nice. The Flower Parade or *Bataille de Fleurs* was added in 1876.

You can read more about the Nice Carnival in my book, "French Holidays & Traditions."

Socca

⁓∞⁓

A Niçois Superfood

Most regions in France have their own gastronomic specialties, and Nice is no exception. Ask anyone what the Niçois specialty is and the answer will be – *socca*.

What is this amazing food that has protected the city under siege, nourished the population during peacetime and inspired men to go to extraordinary lengths to protect it? You might be surprised to know that it's an unassuming chickpea pancake called *socca*.

Socca has been associated with the city of Nice for hundreds of years. In fact, according to one legend, the recipe was discovered when the Turks were attacking the city in 1543 (the same battle in which Catherine Ségurane exhibited her bravery). When they ran out of ammunition, the Niçois mixed hot oil with chickpea soup and poured it down on the heads of the invaders. Apparently, it stopped the Turks and when the defenders licked their fingers they thought – "Hey, this stuff is pretty good! We could probably even sell it!"

It was in the early 1900s (when *socca* was no longer needed for military purposes) that it really started to gain popularity as a quick snack sold from portable ovens. These could be taken to the port in the early morning for the fishermen, then later in the day, rolled over to where other laborers were working. It was nourishing and inexpensive Niçois fast food.

One enterprising Niçoise lady named Térésa set up her *socca* kiosk in Cours Saleya market in 1928 and became something of a legend. It seems that she was a gregarious woman who talked to everyone and was always ready to give her opinion about anything and everything, whether it was solicited or not.

Of course, the original Térésa is no longer in the market, but her place has been taken by another "Térésa." If you visit Cours Saleya today, you will see a stall called "Chez Térésa" where they serve up *socca* that is cooked a few streets away. It arrives by scooter every 5 minutes or so.

Three families have owned this business since the original Térésa was there in 1928. And interestingly, each time it seems that there has been a "woman of character" who slips easily into the role. The one who is there now appears to be more subdued than the one who was there in the 1970s. Christian Gallo relates a story about the 1970s Térésa in his book, *Les Dessous de la Côte*.

In the 1960s and 1970s, the Cours Saleya market was covered and cars were not allowed in the perimeter during market hours. One day an unlucky Parisian in a little Fiat 500 tried to drive through. Finding his way blocked by the merchandise and sellers, he started to honk and rev the engine. This sent exhaust fumes in the direction of Térésa's *socca* – big mistake. She called out to two stout

men nearby and said, "Get that thing away from my *socca*." They picked up the small car and set it down in a tiny street where the driver couldn't even open the doors to get out. He escaped through the roof and probably (if he was smart) waited until the market was closed before going back for his car. I imagine that he showed more respect for *socca* after that.

Today, this humble pancake still plays an important part in Niçois life and can be found in many restaurants in the Old Town. It's a versatile food which can be eaten as a mid-morning snack, a light meal, or an aperitif.

Socca is made in a big round, flat copper pan and cooked in a pizza oven and is best eaten piping hot, dusted with black pepper and accompanied by a glass of rosé.

What to See

♦ **Socca delivery** – In the Cours Saleya market, Chez Térésa is located near the Miséricorde Chapel. *Socca* is delivered to the stall every five minutes or so on a specially equipped socca scooter that has a place for the large *socca* pan and a big conical lid to protect the pancake and keep it piping hot.

♦ **Socca tasting** – Try different *socca* sellers to find your favorite socca. Some people have strong opinions about who makes the best *socca*.

Fun Facts

♦ **Siege of the castle** – The castle on the hill was impenetrable for hundreds of years and withstood many a siege. Some say that the Niçois were able to endure these long sieges because they had large stores of chickpea flour and olive oil which was all they needed to make socca – and the Niçois could happily live on nothing but socca for a long time.

More Niçois
Specialties

∽

What's for Lunch?

Besides the socca that we've already talked about, there are several other Niçois specialties you might want to try.

Salade Niçoise – There has been quite a controversy in Nice since a French TV chef (not from Nice) added green beans and boiled potatoes to what he called a *Salade Niçoise*. The city rose up in protest and almost everyone in Nice offered their recipe for a "real Niçoise salad," and as it turns out, there's no such thing. However, certain "rules" were established.

First of all, everyone agreed that the only cooked items to go in a Niçoise salad are boiled eggs and cooked tuna – but definitely no cooked vegetables. Otherwise you can use your judgment for *most* other vegetables. There is no lettuce and the general consensus is that cucumbers are to be avoided as well.

Remember Jacques Médecin, the mayor of Nice who was facing corruption charges and had to escape to Uruguay (in the Casino Wars story)? Before his problems with the law, he published a Niçois cookbook that his Niçoise grandmother dictated to him. It's still quite popular today. His Niçoise salad recipe is below:

Niçoise salad according to Jacques Médecin (or his grandmother): tomato, cucumber (controversial), artichoke, broad beans, green pepper, onions, olives, garlic, hard-boiled egg, basil, tuna or anchovies (not both), radish (optional) olive oil, salt, and pepper. No vinegar, no lettuce, no cooked vegetables.

Pan bagnat – This sandwich is basically a Niçoise salad on a big bun. A "real" pan bagnat should not have any lettuce or mayonnaise. The name means "wet bread or bathing bread" because many years ago, it was made from stale bread (Waste not want not as my grandmother used to say). The stale bread would be softened up with water before adding the other ingredients. Today crusty, fresh bread is used (as far as we know) and the bread is rubbed with garlic before being filled with the "official" Niçoise salad ingredients.

Pissaladière – An onion tart with *lots* of onions and an anchovy or sardine sauce.

Fougasse/Fougassette – A thin bread with cut-out sections which comes in various shapes. In days gone by, it was used by the bakers to test the heat of their ovens before they baked their "real bread." Then it would be eaten as a snack by the bakers or given out to customers in addition to a bread purchase. Today it has earned its own place on the bakery shelf. You can find plain fougasse, or it can be flavored with olives, tomatoes, cheese, etc. There's also a sweet version flavored with fruit, known as the fougassette.

Tourte de blette – A sweet and sour dessert made of chard (the blette), cheese, raisins, and fruit.

Other specialties to discover: les petits farcis, la daube niçoise, ratatouille niçoise, la soupe au pistou...

NIÇOISE SALAD

Remember:

- No cooked vegetables
- No lettuce

Anthem of Nice

Nissa la Bella

Nissa la Bella (*Nice la Belle* in French and Nice the Beautiful in English) is the anthem of Nice. It was written in Niçois in 1903 by Menica Rondelly. Below is my attempt at its translation.

Nice the Beautiful

Viva, viva Nice the beautiful!

Oh my beautiful Nice,
Queen of all flowers,
Of your ancient rooftops
I will forever sing.
I will sing of your mountains,
Of your rich scenery,
Your green countryside,
Your large golden sun.

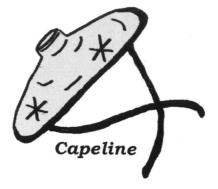

Capeline

Forever I will sing
Under your bowers,
Of your azure sea,
Your sky so pure.
And forever I will proclaim
In my refrain,
Viva, viva Nice the beautiful!

I will sing of the capeline[1],
The rose and the lilac,
The Port and the Marina,
Paillon[2], Mascoïnat[3]!
I will sing of the garret
Where songs are born,
Of the spindle, the distaff,
My beautiful Nanon

1.   The traditional, flat, wide-brimmed hat worn by Niçoise ladies.
2.   The river that runs under the Promenade du Paillon.
3.   An area in the Old Town.

Flag of Nice

I will sing of our glories,
The ancient and beautiful Roman lantern[4],
The victories of the castle[5],
The scent of your springtime!
I will sing of the ancient Sincaire[6],
Your white flag[7] unfurled,
And the birthplace of my mother,
The most beautiful in the world.

4.   Possibly a reference to Cimiez which was a Roman city.
5.   The castle (or fortress) that stood on the *Colline du Château*.
6.   Sincaire means five-sided and is the name of a street where a five-sided
     tower once stood. It's also the street with the monument to Nice's heroine,
     Catherine Ségurane.
7.   The flag of Nice bears a red eagle in a shield with a crown above it and
     foliage surrounding it. The eagle stands on three hills over a stylized sea. The
     background is white.

About the Author

Margo Lestz is American by birth but now divides her time between London, England and Nice, France (with a little bit of Florence, Italy thrown in for good measure). Life in a foreign country is never dull and every day is a new learning experience.

She describes herself as a perpetual student and is always taking some kind of course or researching a moment in history that has caught her fancy. She's curious by nature and is always wondering who, what, why, when, where, and how.

Margo shares her adventures (and her questions) with Jeff, her husband of many years.

Nice, France is the second book in her Curious Histories series.

Margo is also the author of: *French Holidays & Traditions*

Author site: margolestz.com
Blog: curiousrambler.com (Curious Rambler)

Manufactured by Amazon.ca
Bolton, ON

17229283R00081